Praise for *The Girl's Guide to NASCAR*

"I wouldn't be surprised if THE GIRL'S GUIDE TO NASCAR became the most coveted book on NASCAR for men, too. NASCAR buff or novice, this book is for anyone hoping to get a better edge on America's fastest-growing sport."

—Roger Staubach, chairman and CEO,
The Staubach Company

"Liz has captured the reality of our business like no one has before—interesting, informative, a book that will complete your NASCAR collection."

—Jeff Hammond, Fox Sports

"This is an extremely entertaining inside look at the sport."

—Rusty Wallace, 55 NASCAR Winston (Nextel) Cup wins,
36 career Winston Cup pole positions

"An enjoyable read with some good information and tips for the 'Girls.'"

—Bobby Allison, 1983 NASCAR Winston (Nextel) Cup champion,
85 cup wins, third most wins in NASCAR racing

"I've never seen a book that explains so much of the technical side of NASCAR in such a fun way."

—Benny Parsons, NASCAR Winston Cup Series champion
and commentator for NBC and TNT

"Liz Allison has seen the sport of NASCAR from every angle—good and bad. I can't think of a better person to give the ladies the inside scoop."

—Larry McReynolds, two-time Daytona 500 winning crew chief,
broadcast analyst for *NASCAR on Fox*

The Girl's Guide to

Liz Allison

Foreword by Darrell Waltrip

CENTER
STREET

New York   Boston   Nashville

The information provided in this book is based on sources that the author believes to be reliable. All such information regarding individual products and companies is current as of September 2005.

The opinions expressed in this book are solely those of the author and do not necessarily reflect the views of NASCAR, its employees, or its representatives.

Copyright © 2006 by Liz Allison
Foreword copyright © 2006 by Darrell Waltrip
All rights reserved. No part of this book may be reproduced in any form or by any electronic or mechanical means, including information storage and retrieval systems, without permission in writing from the publisher, except by a reviewer who may quote brief passages in a review.

Center Street
Time Warner Book Group
1271 Avenue of the Americas, New York, NY 10020
Visit our Web site at www.twbookmark.com.

Center Street and the Center Street logo are registered trademarks of Time Warner Book Group Inc.

NASCAR and the NASCAR Library Collection are registered trademarks of the National Association for Stock Car Auto Racing, Inc.

Printed in the United States of America
First Edition: May 2006
10 9 8 7 6 5 4 3 2 1

Library of Congress Cataloging-in-Publication Data

Allison, Liz.
     The girl's guide to NASCAR / Liz Allison.— 1st ed.
        p.   cm.
     ISBN-13: 978-1-931722-71-1
     ISBN-10: 1-931722-71-4
     1. Stock car racing.   2. Stock car racing—Terminology.   3. NASCAR (Association).
I. Title.

     GV1029.9.S74A55   2006
     796.72—dc22   2005023962

Writing this book was similar to being on a race team in the fact that it took many people behind the scenes to get the job done. Without my crew, this book would not be possible.

Crew chief—Krista. Thank you for sharing your God-given talents with this project. You truly are the MVP. I am so amazed by your natural creative abilities.

Car chief—Larry McReynolds. Thank you for serving as my on-call guy. You never tire of talking shop . . . thank goodness. I appreciate you always being there for me, no matter what the situation. You are the best!

Chief engine builder—Russ Thompson. Wow, your knowledge of the sport of auto racing blows me away. Thank you for sharing your memory bank with me. Your passion for racing, combined with your vast knowledge, makes you a true racing champion.

Spotter—Ryan. You are my second set of eyes and ears. You always know how to "steer" me when I am "off track." Thank you for your unending support.

Team manager—Pamela Harty. Thank you for guiding me through all of the ins and outs of the book world. I would be "in the pits" without your leadership. Your genuine support is a rare find.

Car owners—Christina Boys and Chip MacGregor with Center Street. Thank you for believing in me as your driver. This has been the "best ride" anyone could ask for. Christina, thank you for allowing me to bring your idea and title to reality.

Tire specialist—Robbie. Thank you for always being honest. I love that you let me know when I have a "flat." Your complete honesty sent me back to the table many times to "better the grip."

General mechanic—Sweet Baby Bella. Thank you for your "generalized" happiness. You always have a smile and a giggle to share. What a gift you are!

The over-the-wall gang—All of my dear friends who allowed me to be a "deadbeat" friend during the six weeks it took to write this book . . . thank you. No driver is worth a cent without the crew to back them up. You all are my rock.

Primary sponsor—Jen White with NASCAR. It has been a privilege to work with you again. Thanks to you we are "race ready."

Chapter Seven
Race Strategy   53

Chapter Eight
Hey, Baby, That Doesn't Look Like My Ford   61

Chapter Nine
How Safe Can Racing Really Be?   67

Chapter Ten
Rules, What Rules?   77

Part Three: The Nuts and Bolts

When I first met Liz, she was a starry-eyed NASCAR fan hanging out by the back of her future husband's hauler, hoping for a chance to meet the one and only Darrell Waltrip. Always obliging to my fans, I paused to make her day and say hello. Now, eighteen years, four months, and three days later, she has asked me to write the foreword for her new book, *The Girl's Guide to NASCAR*.

Of course, I had to read the manuscript before I'd agree. Since there are "no men allowed" after this foreword, I was only permitted to read the title page. But it is a fine one, and the foreword is superb. Never one to follow other people's rules, however, I have gone where only ladies were permitted, and I have to say this is a great book. I particularly enjoyed the profound comments that appear on pages 27, 51, and 81. I did find it offensive that my name was omitted from the "Sexiest Drivers Over 40" list in chapter 5, but Liz assured me that had this included former champions as well as current drivers my name would have been first on this list. No female knows racing and which drivers are sexiest like Liz.

Women have come a long way in the sport of NASCAR racing. When I first started competing, my wife, Stevie, wasn't allowed in the garage or pit areas and had to watch the race from the grandstands. Now women play a role in every aspect of the sport, from crew members and NASCAR officials to car owners and drivers on the track. There are so many female NASCAR fans that they need their very own book!

I have always found NASCAR to be my favorite sport, particularly because of the many confusing rules that Liz has somehow managed to explain in a way that makes sense in the following pages. (In fact, this book would have come in handy when I was racing.) I have also learned why Stevie was always willing to go with me to the races. I didn't realize how many places there were to shop near the tracks until I saw them listed in this book.

Okay, ladies, it's time for you to venture where only one man has gone before. Boogity boogity boogity!

Darrell Waltrip

3 time Winston Cup champion,
84 wins,
59 poles,
Author of *DW: A Lifetime Going Around in Circles*,
Sexiest former driver in NASCAR*

* Polled by 30 million female NASCAR fans

CAUTION

FOR LADIES ONLY—NO MEN ALLOWED!

Liz Allison Meets NASCAR

I am quite convinced that Summerville, South Carolina, about fifteen miles outside of Charleston in the heart of the "Low Country," is the hottest place on the face of the earth. It was on a particularly hot and hazy night in August when I found myself down at the Summerville Speedway. My girlfriends had convinced me to come with them to see the "NASCAR boys" who were in town for a celebrity race-off. I was twenty-one, didn't have a care in the world, and certainly couldn't miss seeing the NASCAR boys . . . the only problem was I wouldn't have known one if he were standing in front of me.

Every year the NASCAR drivers came to town for the Tiny Lund Memorial. Tiny was a driver killed at Talladega Superspeedway in 1975, and the event was an annual fund-raiser for his wife, Wanda, and son, Chris.

I guess you could say that I was a new fan to the sport. I knew a little about racing, but not quite as much as I thought. I found that to be a fact very soon after my initial meeting with the man who would (eventually) become my husband.

I had worn shorts and a T-shirt to weather the heat, and couldn't help noticing a tall, dark, and (somewhat) handsome stranger approaching me dressed all in black. Black corduroy pants, black golf shirt, black long-sleeved jacket . . . was he out of his mind? He looked like he was ready for a New England winter, not a sultry Low Country summer. Not to mention, he was either the biggest Texaco Havoline fan in the world, or maybe (just maybe) he had just won a giveaway at the local gas station, because everything he had on was covered in the Texaco logo.

He ambled over to me, jumped up on the back of the truck where I was standing, and introduced himself as (to my surprise) . . . Davey Allison. I had heard of

Davey Allison before, mainly because he was the son of legendary racer Bobby Allison. Davey was an up-and-coming driver on the Winston Cup circuit. I did not know much about him other than that his face was on every magazine cover and sports section of the newspaper, so he was doing something right.

He commented about the nice weather we were having in the "Boiling" Country. I knew at that very moment that he must be off his rocker. It was *only* a *mere* 98 degrees outside, and, I am sure, the most humid night EVER! Despite this, somehow he got my attention. It could have been the heat, but I think it was the deep brown eyes. Whatever it was, my life would never be the same. I am sure you have heard "you had me at hello." Well, he had me at hello.

This would be the start of my life in NASCAR.

My inaugural Cup race as a racer's girlfriend was not the best showing of a "seasoned" race fan. It was November 1988, Atlanta Motor Speedway. I really thought I knew something about racing until I realized that not only did I not know how to tell who was leading a race, but I couldn't figure out what they meant when they said a car was "a lap down." They all looked like they were racing together to me. My seasoned-race-fan status dropped another ten notches when I asked the goofy question, "How can Davey be running sixth when there are ten cars in front of him?"

It occurred to me at that moment that I must either figure out this sport or sit it out. I chose to figure it out, but not without a few minor (and major) crashes along the way. Penalties, testing, qualifying, black flags . . . my head was spinning just at the thought of this amazing and quite exciting sport that was *so very confusing*.

Confusing as it may be, once you get the basics, you will be ready for the big leagues. What I have learned about NASCAR is that no matter how much things change, one thing stays the same—the rich culture of the sport.

I will share with you in the following pages what I have learned through my hard knocks of living the NASCAR life. I will teach you the history of a sport that has grown beyond (I believe) even NASCAR founder Bill France Sr.'s vision for the sport over half a century ago. I will even give you tips on throwing your own NASCAR viewing party and on traveling to and from race events. Believe it or not, there is much more to do at races than just watch the race.

During my seventeen years in the sport my role has changed significantly, but my love and passion for NASCAR racing has never faded. When I lost my husband, and the racing world lost a fierce competitor, in 1993, I decided to take a step back until the wounds could heal. After a few years, the fire was reignited inside me for the sport that I love. I came back home, if you will, as a member of the sports media covering NASCAR in print, radio, and television.

I hope that my journey and zest for racing will enlighten your racing know-how. Racing is a fun and competitive sport. Be ready to catch the fever, because once you are a fan . . . you are always a fan.

Okay, ladies, sit back, read, laugh, and enjoy my NASCAR guide for the girls. I guarantee I will have you ready to talk NASCAR with the most knowledgeable race fan. Let's go racing!

PART ONE

NASCAR 101

CHAPTER ONE

The Starting Lineup

The popularity and growth of the sport speaks for itself. But make no mistake, the National Association for Stock Car Auto Racing (NASCAR) has carefully charted and directed the course of the enormously successful stock car racing series from the very beginning. The NASCAR you see today seems to be very different from the NASCAR that started over fifty years ago, but it is not as different as one might think. What has remained "on track" through the years are the colorful personalities of the drivers, the fierce competition, and the steadfast fans.

Before NASCAR

Was there wheeled racing before NASCAR? You betcha . . . but not what we know as racing in this day and age. Racing can be traced back as far as the horse-and-buggy days when young men (and women) with a need for speed rumbled across rock-filled dirt roads. Later generations raced cars on back roads and makeshift drag strips before the first racetrack was ever built. The first racetracks were simply dirt, making for great racing and dirt-filled noses and ears. The beauty of the racing of years past was the concept of "from the road to the track." Basically, if you had four wheels, you could race. It was not uncommon to have your dentist and milkman racing each other on Saturday night at the local racetrack. It would be years before the word "professional" would come before "race car driver." Until then, racing was a fun hobby for thrill seekers; certainly nothing like the big business it is today.

The Indianapolis Motor Speedway, completed in 1909, was technically the first non-dirt track to be built in the United States, even though it did not run stock cars at first. The track surface was built out of bricks instead of asphalt . . . 3.2 million bricks, to be exact, hence the nickname the Brickyard.

Professional auto racing began with a jumbled array of small sanctioning bodies for stock car racing across the Southeast that organized races from the mid-1930s until the late 1940s. There was no governing body or anyone to basically police the events, setting the stage for several different problems for the drivers . . . like being paid, for example. Before NASCAR, a race promoter might set up a race, raise the funds for the race purse, sell tickets, bring in the drivers, and then head out of town before the race was over—with the winnings, ticket monies, and all. Many racers were left with nothing but expenses and no paycheck to help pay the bills.

Undoubtedly, NASCAR racing would be in a different place if not for the vision of a banker turned race car driver from Washington, D.C., by the name of Bill France. Seeking his dreams, France had set out on a cross-country trip from Washington to Miami when a little car trouble sidetracked him for a few days in Daytona Beach, Florida. That unplanned stopover changed the course of his life and the course of racing.

France—The Founding Family

NASCAR was founded in Daytona Beach, Florida, on December 14, 1947, by William H. G. France. He stood six and a half feet tall, earning himself the nickname "Big Bill." Many thought his stature illuminated an intimidating nature, but the people who knew him best felt that his toughness was only for show; his soft side was saved for those who were closest to him. Bill's vision far exceeded anything the world of racing had ever known. Being a driver himself, he understood the ins and outs of the sport. He wanted to take it to the big leagues, in hopes of one day making it mainstream. His interest in television and radio coverage was laughed off by many businessmen, who only saw it as a wild dream.

On December 14, 1947, Mr. France called a meeting at the Streamline Hotel in what is now the world center of racing, Daytona Beach. There he convinced business associates and investors to follow his dream. Just a few short months later on February 15, 1948, the France dream became a reality as NASCAR ran its first race on the beach at Daytona. The first-ever NASCAR event was won by the racing legend Red Byron. Only six days later NASCAR was incorporated. The world of racing would never be the same.

The first Strictly Stock race (what we know today as the Nextel Cup Series) was run at the Charlotte Fairgrounds Speedway in North Carolina on June 19, 1949.

Soon afterward, racers started flocking in from around the country, making Charlotte another hub for racing. This remains the case today, as most teams are based out of the Charlotte area. Red Byron was crowned the very first NASCAR champion that October. His six starts and two wins in 1949 afforded him $5,800 in winnings.

Bill Sr. decided to change the name of NASCAR's top series subtitle in 1950 from Strictly Stock to Grand National, and from 1950 to 1959 NASCAR continued its growth in popularity, finally catching the attention of executives at CBS Sports. January 31, 1960 marked the first live televised race coverage on any network, as the *CBS Sports Spectacular* broadcast a two-hour program devoted to the Daytona pole-qualifying events. ABC Sports followed the lead of CBS by including the July 16, 1960, Firecracker 250 in their *Wide World of Sports* programming.

History was made in 1971 when the RJ Reynolds Tobacco Company, the parent company of Winston cigarettes, announced its plans to become the first title sponsor of the growing Grand National Division of NASCAR racing. Cigarette advertising was undergoing major changes, as the marketing of tobacco products was banned from television, leaving an insane amount of unused advertising dollars lying on the table. The RJR Company initially went to legendary racer and car owner Junior Johnson to sponsor his race team. Junior, realizing very quickly that RJR's financial support far exceeded anything he could use, steered the powerhouse tobacco company to NASCAR, whose elite series was renamed the Winston Cup Grand National Division. This would forge one of the longest-standing relationships in the history of the sport.

Fast Fact

What we now know as the Nextel Cup Series has had many names over the years. Even though the name of the series has changed, NASCAR has always been the sanctioning body.

1949–1950	Strictly Stock
1950–1971	Grand National
1971–1986	Winston Cup Grand National Division
1986–2003	Winston Cup Series
2004–present	Nextel Cup Series*

*Nextel and Sprint merged in 2005, which could result in a name change in the foreseeable future.

The Fight

As the laps were winding down in the 1979 Daytona 500, tempers were flaring up. On the last lap of the race Donnie Allison was leading, with Cale Yarborough on his back bumper. Cale dove down to make a pass while Donnie was attempting to hold him off, and as the two fought over Daytona real estate, they got together and wrecked in Turn 3. The King, Richard Petty, went on to capture one of his seven Daytona 500 titles. After the checkered flag waved, as Petty made his way to Victory Lane, Donnie Allison and Yarborough argued on the grass in Turn 3. Donnie's brother, Bobby, also a 500 competitor, stopped his car and joined in what has become one of the most talked-about moments in NASCAR history . . . known simply as The Fight.

In 1972, at the age of sixty-three, Bill Sr. passed the torch to his son William C. France, more commonly known as Bill Jr. Bill Sr. had been molding his son for several years, waiting for the day he felt Bill Jr. was ready to take NASCAR into the next generation. Bill Jr. became the second president of NASCAR. By this time, NASCAR racing was making its way all over the southeastern states, from South Carolina to Virginia and just about every state in between, and Bill Jr. felt it necessary to trim the Winston Cup Grand National Division schedule from forty-eight to thirty-one races. His plan was to focus more attention on the growth of fewer tracks, and to put some distance between the tracks. This was the birth of the modern era of NASCAR.

CBS Sports made history on February 18, 1979, as the network gave flag-to-flag live coverage of the Daytona 500. The King—Richard Petty—won the coveted trophy after an infamous wreck between Cale Yarborough and Donnie Allison. This wild finish produced one of the most replayed events in the history of the sport.

The growth of the sport and its popularity kept the attention of the networks, who chose sporadic events to cover throughout the course of each race season. In 1989, NASCAR had earned enough credibility and respect that the networks granted coverage to every NASCAR Winston Cup event, broadcasting them on national or cable TV.

Bill France Sr. passed away in 1992, leaving the creation and growth of NASCAR as his legacy. By the time NASCAR's fiftieth anniversary arrived in 1998, Bill France Jr. was ready to hand over day-to-day duties to Mike Helton, who was at that time the senior vice president and chief operating officer. History was made on November 28, 2000, when Bill Jr. officially named Helton the third president of NASCAR, making him the first (and only) person outside of the France family to lead the way.

As Helton had been groomed for many years to take the lead of NASCAR, so had Bill Jr.'s son, Brian Z. France. In October 2003, Brian became the chairman of the board and CEO of NASCAR, replacing his father.

Meanwhile, the more than thirty-year relationship between Winston and NASCAR came to an end, and it was announced on June 19, 2003, that Nextel would take the title sponsor lead. The Nextel Cup Series kicked off its first event in February 2004.

Brian France made waves early in 2004 when he introduced a change in the

The Men and Women Behind NASCAR

Chairman of the board and chief executive officer—Brian Z. France
Vice chairman—Bill France Jr.
Vice chairman/executive vice president—James C. France (brother of Bill Jr.)
Member, NASCAR board of directors—Lesa France Kennedy
President—Mike Helton
Chief operating officer—George Pyne
Chief financial officer—Todd Wilson
Assistant secretary—Betty Jane France (wife of Bill Jr.)
Senior vice president—Paul Brooks
Vice president, corporate administration–Ed Bennett
Vice president, corporate communications—Jim Hunter
Vice president, licensing consumer products—Mark Dyer
Vice president, broadcasting and news media—Richard Glover
Vice president, competition—Robin Pemberton
Vice president, research and development—Gary Nelson
Director of diversity and special projects—Tish Sheets
NASCAR Nextel Cup Series director—John Darby
NASCAR Busch Series director—Joe Balash
NASCAR Craftsman Truck Series director—Wayne Auton

Board of Directors

Brian France—chairman
Bill France Jr.—vice chairman
Jim France—vice chairman
Mike Helton
George Pyne
Lesa France Kennedy

way the sport's top series would run its competitive schedule. Beginning at Daytona in February 2004, only the top ten drivers, or those drivers within 400 points of the points leader, would compete in the final ten races leading to the Cup, which ultimately produced one of the most exciting championship battles in the history of the sport. Leading into the final event of the 2004 season, five drivers positioned themselves to have a shot at being the NASCAR Nextel Cup champion. Many believed that the championship battle had become boring and stagnant in years past, but that notion was put to rest as the final laps wound down in the final race of 2004. Kurt Busch won his first title by a mere twelve inches.

You might be a female NASCAR fan if . . .

You get a special "Jeff Gordon" paint scheme on your toenails.

The NASCAR that was formed more than fifty years ago by Brian's grandfather Bill Sr. is gone but not forgotten. The idea is the same, the competition factor is the same, but the approach is big mainstream business. The sport has been given a new face, and this generation has become known as the "new" NASCAR.

The Popularity and Growth of the Sport

For many, the thrill of racing has always been an enticing phenomenon. It is hard not to get excited by the highly competitive races NASCAR hosts in this day and age. NASCAR has the extensive TV and radio coverage to thank for the ever-growing number of race fans. But what made the sport so contagious years before the media coverage? The silent bug . . . *the need for speed.*

Girlfriend to Girlfriend

Let's face it, ladies, NASCAR drivers are pretty darn cute. There is just something about a guy in uniform that makes you want to take him home to Momma.

That "need for speed" seems to live dormant in many of us until someone or something brings it to the surface. Do you remember the first time you came off your couch yelling for your favorite driver to win or the time you could have punched the lights out of another driver for taking your driver out of the race?

Now you've got it.

Some 75 million fans around the country have decided the "need for speed" is what plants them in front of a TV every weekend to watch the best racing there is. NASCAR racing is contagious; once you get "bit by the bug," you are history! This virus is making NASCAR the fastest-growing sport in the country.

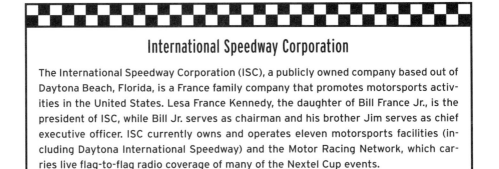

International Speedway Corporation

The International Speedway Corporation (ISC), a publicly owned company based out of Daytona Beach, Florida, is a France family company that promotes motorsports activities in the United States. Lesa France Kennedy, the daughter of Bill France Jr., is the president of ISC, while Bill Jr. serves as chairman and his brother Jim serves as chief executive officer. ISC currently owns and operates eleven motorsports facilities (including Daytona International Speedway) and the Motor Racing Network, which carries live flag-to-flag radio coverage of many of the Nextel Cup events.

Who Are the Fans, Anyway?

NASCAR fans are people just like you and me who love the sport of stock car racing. There are an estimated 75 million race fans from every walk of life, and more than 250 million people view NASCAR events each year. Amazingly, 40 percent of those fans are women. The younger-generation drivers and the so-called hotties of NASCAR have made the sport more attractive to the younger fan as well as the female fan, and female and child-age fans make up its fastest-growing demographics. It is not uncommon to have every family member pull for a different driver, and the brand loyalty of NASCAR fans is second to none. It is estimated that an astounding 72 percent of NASCAR fans consciously select the products of NASCAR sponsors.

Girlfriend to Girlfriend

Contrary to the opinions of many, NASCAR fans are not toothless rednecks who can't read or write. Female NASCAR fans are educated women who simply love the competition NASCAR displays, as well as the many personalities of the drivers who compete in the Cup Series. Some even wear Lilly Pulitzer and pearls!

CHAPTER TWO

Let's Go to the Races

The NASCAR season is long and grueling. The opener in Daytona kicks off in mid-February, and the season finale takes place in mid-November at Homestead-Miami. Testing for the new season begins in January, so as you can see, there is not much time off for race car drivers. The so called off-season is a joke among the drivers—there is virtually no "off" time. NASCAR has one of the longest-running seasons of any organized sport in the United States, with the Nextel Cup season consisting of thirty-six point race events and three non-points events. This treacherous schedule only allows three weekends off from February until November.

NASCAR's Top Three

NASCAR racing is based on a ladder system. What this means basically is that you cannot wake up one day and drive to your closest Nextel Cup event with a race car and expect to race. There is a system in place that polices the events and the drivers who participate. NASCAR determines when a driver is ready for the next step, or, rather, the next series.

After a driver has made it through one of the NASCAR training grounds like the Dodge Weekly Series, the AutoZone Elite Division, the Grand National Division, or the Featherlite Modified Series, he or she must be approved by NASCAR to go any further. The most popular series for young up-and-coming drivers is the Craftsman Truck Series. The old saying, "See you on the way up and back on the way down," fits this series: many drivers start their careers in the trucks and end their career in the trucks. NASCAR has the final word on whether a driver is ready to advance to the next series. This is to keep drivers who are inexperienced from endangering themselves or someone else. All of the NASCAR series are run off of a points system. Just about everything in NASCAR comes down to points. The championship is determined by points, as are many other facets of the sport. The bottom line is, the better off you are in points, the better off you are, period.

The Craftsman Truck Series

The Truck Series is the newest to join the NASCAR family. The first Truck Series race was run on February 5, 1995, at Phoenix International Raceway. Mike Skinner won the inaugural event. This series has become a great training ground for young drivers hoping to one day race on the Cup level. More recently, it has become a second home for veteran Cup drivers looking to trim back their hectic schedules. Forty-seven-year-old Bobby Hamilton won the Craftsman Truck Series title in 2004, after leaving a full-time Cup ride to compete full-time in the trucks. The Truck Series runs a much lighter schedule than the other two series, with only twenty-five main events. An informal name for this series is the "Seniors Tour."

Busch Whackers

The widely used phrase "Busch Whackers" refers to the full-time Cup drivers who choose to race the Busch race on Saturday. Many Busch drivers feel the Cup drivers have an unfair advantage during Busch events. Hence the name. The Cup drivers whack the Busch field, stealing wins from them as well as a big chunk of the race winnings.

Many drivers and race fans alike feel the Truck Series provides the best races week in and week out and the truck events have grown more popular than many critics thought possible. One reason for this is that the races are shorter in length, which basically means the drivers have to get to the front quicker. The trucks seem to beat and bang a little more, providing action-packed racing for the fans. It is also less expensive to run a team in truck racing, leaving the door open to many sponsors who cannot dish out the high dollars needed to race in the Cup Series.

The Busch Series

The Busch Series was originated in 1950, originally known as the NASCAR Sportsman Division. A relationship with Anheiser-Busch was conceived in 1982. Although the name of the series has changed several times through the course of the long-standing relationship with Anheiser-Busch, NASCAR's second most popular series still carries the Busch name today. Many young drivers use it as a training ground for the Cup Series. Busch Series races are run on many of the same tracks as the Cup events, making this a good place to learn the tricks of the trade. The Busch Series consists of thirty-five events a season, making participants' travel schedule almost as rigorous as that of the Cup Series teams. Many Cup drivers compete in the Busch Series on Cup companion race weekends, which occur when the Busch and Cup series races are at the same track on the same weekend. The Busch cars race on Saturday and the Cup cars race on Sunday.

The Nextel Cup Series

This series, which runs thirty-six point races a year, features an elite group of drivers who have reached the top of the sport of stock car racing. These are the best stock car racers in the world—names like Dale Earnhardt Jr., Jeff Gordon, Jimmie Johnson, and Kurt Busch. Most racers only dream of racing at this level. These drivers are the best of the best! Every one of them has worked long and hard to make it to the top, having raced for many years and being cleared by NASCAR to race on the tracks that host Cup events. Every driver competing on the Cup level races for championship points, although many drivers are not in contention for the actual championship due to lack of impressive finishes. Rookie drivers (see more on rookies on page 41) have different guidelines to follow than non-rookie drivers. Each year one driver is awarded the championship trophy and the title of NASCAR Nextel Cup champion, an honor most drivers can only dream of. Most professional drivers race their entire careers trying just to make it to the Cup Series.

Saturday Night Fever

Night racing is the hottest thing going in NASCAR! So what makes night racing so exciting? It's like local Friday night racing . . . Anytown, USA.

The drivers you see racing every week on the NASCAR Cup circuit didn't just wake up one day and decide to be race car drivers. Nextel Cup drivers are the elite top dogs of the stock car racing world. They all have one thing in common: they learned to race at a local track somewhere, and they all learned the ropes in local nighttime racing.

There is just something about being at a racetrack in the evening that is completely invigorating. Let me tell you, when the sun goes down in NASCAR and the lights turn on, something strange happens to the drivers . . . something ignites inside them that sends electricity through the grandstands. And the race fans catch the fever.

Night racing is becoming more and more popular, with more tracks adding

Girlfriend to Girlfriend

Nicknames for the Cup Series drivers include: the big boys, the Sunday drivers, the Cup boys, the Nextel boys.

The Top Five . . .

Must-See Tracks—You Won't Believe Your Eyes

1. Bristol
2. Daytona
3. Lowe's Motor Speedway (Charlotte)
4. Talladega
5. Indy

*Girlfriend
to Girlfriend*

The night races that happen to fall on a full moon are not soon forgotten. It is a known fact that full moon races have more cautions, wrecks, and controversy than any others. Hence the saying, "The drivers are howling at the moon."

lights each year. This may be a timely addition, but it's quite expensive, estimated to cost anywhere from $2 to $6 million. Tracks like Phoenix, Homestead-Miami, and Darlington have added lights in the past few years.

As prime-time TV wars continue and the popularity of night racing continues to grow, expect more races to be under the lights.

The Tracks—Inside and Out

The tracks on the Cup circuit were not built exclusively for NASCAR Cup events. Keep in mind that a track hosts two Cup events a season (at best). That leaves many months of disuse if the track does not host other racing events from other forms of auto racing. Each racetrack is unique in and of itself. Some have flatter, wider race surfaces, while others are more narrow and banked. As each track is different in its layout, so are the degree of banking and number of laps run for an event. A track's banking is based on what type of cars will be run on it.

Take a non-Cup track like Nashville, which hosts two NASCAR Busch Series races each season along with a Truck Series event as well as an Indy Racing League (IRL) race. Tracks have to make money the best way they can, and that is to make the track raceable for as many types of cars as possible.

A track like Bristol, on the other hand, has 36 degrees banked in the turns and therefore could not host an Indy car. However, the severe banking creates some of the best racing of the year for the Cup cars. The average banking for the majority of the tracks is 14 degrees. This allows most any type of race machine to perform

---

NASCAR Nextel Cup Series Cars versus Indy Racing League (IRL) Cars

Cup cars are based on the principle of a production car, basically off the assembly line. A Cup car weighs 3,400 pounds (without the driver) and averages 185 mph.

Indy cars, in contrast, are purpose-built racing machines, meaning they are built only for racing. They weigh 1,500 pounds and average 230 mph.

Many tracks on the Cup circuit also hosts IRL events. Richmond, Texas, Fontana, Kansas, Chicagoland, Indy, Phoenix, Homestead, Michigan, Watkins Glen, and Sonoma (Infineon) are all tracks that welcome both forms of racing at least once a year.

safely. Even though Bristol is a very popular Cup event twice a year, it is very limited in other racing events due to the severity of its banking.

NASCAR Cup Series events are hosted on four different types of track: short track, intermediate track, superspeedway, and road course. Most drivers find a certain style of track more conducive to their driving style, making them "specialists" on those particular tracks. Dale Earnhardt Jr. is known for his restrictor-plate race success, while drivers like Elliott Sadler and Kurt Busch excel on short tracks.

The Top Five ...

Most Exciting Tracks to Watch a Race

1. Bristol
2. Martinsville
3. Darlington
4. Daytona
5. Atlanta

Fast Fact

NASCAR races are an average of three and a half hours long. Network television allows a four-hour window for the full race with pre-race and post-race interviews. Some drivers, such as Kyle Petty, feel the races are too long. The longest race of the season is the Coca-Cola 600 at Lowe's Motor Speedway in Charlotte. This marathon event starts late in the afternoon but many times doesn't finish until almost midnight. It is especially tough on the drivers; it's basically a "race till you drop." Why make it so long? So that each event is different. The number of laps for any NASCAR event is set by the individual track promoters along with NASCAR.

Very few drivers have found the "golden ticket" to all four styles of tracks on the NASCAR circuit. The true sign of a champion racer is one who can succeed on all the tracks NASCAR has included in the current schedule. Drivers like retired champions David Pearson and Richard Petty were able to find the checkered flag regardless of what style track the race was on. Jeff Gordon is the most successful current driver in all forms of NASCAR racing. He has won on almost every NASCAR track on the Cup circuit, leaving competitors scratching their heads at his ability to adapt to the track at hand.

Girlfriend to Girlfriend

The fact that Jeff Gordon can race (and win) on virtually any style track makes him a championship contender almost every year. Drivers like Gordon are extremely tough to beat week in and week out because of their "across the board" driving ability.

Short Tracks—Beating and Banging

Description—Tracks less than one mile in length.

Tracks—Bristol, Martinsville, and Richmond.

Characteristics—Less track . . . more tempers! The track size makes for a very exciting race, with lots of cautions and lots of hot tempers.

Who's hot—Kurt Busch, Dale Earnhardt Jr., Jeff Gordon, Jimmie Johnson, Tony Stewart.

Intermediate Tracks—The In-Betweens

Description—Tracks more than one mile but not more than two miles in length.

Tracks—Atlanta, California, Chicagoland, Darlington, Dover, Homestead, Kansas, Vegas, Lowe's (Charlotte), New Hampshire, Michigan, Phoenix, Pocono, Texas.

Characteristics—More tracks make up this group than any other style track in the series. All of these tracks are different in size and shape.

Who's hot—Greg Biffle, Carl Edwards, Jeff Gordon, Dale Jarrett, Jimmie Johnson, Matt Kenseth, Ryan Newman.

Superspeedways—The Big Boys

Description—Tracks more than two miles in length.

Tracks—Pocono, Indy, Talladega,* Daytona.*

Characteristics—The term "wide open" comes from superspeedway racing. Most drivers learn their skills on short tracks, making the bigger tracks tougher to tame.

Who's hot—Dale Earnhardt Jr., Jeff Gordon, Jimmie Johnson, Tony Stewart, Michael Waltrip.

Road Courses—Twists and Turns

Description—Tracks that are irregular in shape, with hairpin-shaped turns and both left and right turns, like a real road.

Tracks—Infineon, Watkins Glen.

---

*These two superspeedways use restrictor plates (see page 65).

Characteristics—Many drivers and fans dislike this form of racing. The consensus is that road racing has no place in the NASCAR series. Few Cup drivers excel on this style of track, and it is not uncommon to see road-racing specialists from other racing series such as Scott Pruett, Boris Said, and Ron Fellows attemping to qualify and race in these two events.

Who's hot—Jeff Gordon, Robby Gordon, Ricky Rudd, Tony Stewart.

The Points System

NASCAR racing is based on a points system that basically awards the winner the most points and moves down through the field of finishers. Other point bonuses are awarded to any driver who leads a lap and the driver who leads the most laps; anyone who earns either will receive five championship points.

The Top Five . . .

Prettiest Tracks

1. Martinsville
2. Indy
3. Vegas
4. Infineon (Sonoma)
5. Lowe's (Charlotte)

Fast Fact

The most points earned in the modern era (1972–present) was in 1972 by the King himself, Richard Petty. He tallied a total of 8,701.4 championship points by season's end, winning eight races, three poles, and $265,460.

From 1948 to 1972 (premodern era) the most points earned was in 1967, also by Richard Petty. He finished the season with 42,472 championship points, twenty-seven wins, nineteen poles, and $130,275 in winnings.

The winner of each race receives 180 points. Then the points are distributed as follows:

2nd 170	9th 138	15th 118
3rd 165	10th 134	16th 115
4th 160	11th 130	17th 112
5th 155	12th 127	18th 109
6th 150	13th 124	19th 106
7th 146	14th 121	20th 103
8th 142		

The remaining points are distributed in three-point increments; the last car in the finishing order (forty-third) receives 34 points.

The Chase Is On

2004 brought a new face to the world of NASCAR Cup Series racing. Brian France felt a strong need to add a playoff system to the Nextel Cup Series that would highlight and bring more attention and excitement to the end of the race season.

The new system basically places the first twenty-six races of the race season as the regular series events, referred to as the "Race for the Chase." The last ten races are known as the Chase for the NASCAR Nextel Cup—or for short, "the Chase."

The top ten drivers in points after the twenty-sixth race of the season, as well as drivers who are within 400 points of the leader, will race for the Cup championship title. Any driver not in the top ten or within 400 points of the leader is not eligible to win the championship. Outside of championship contenders, the best a driver can finish is eleventh.

The Chase for the Championship contenders have their points reset before the ten-race shootout begins, leaving only five points difference between each competitor, starting with 5,050 and working back through the top ten in order to give all the drivers in the championship run a shot at the title. The points are set at 5,050 so that drivers outside of the Chase cannot catch up by accumulating points. Let's say a driver is outside of the top ten when the Chase for the Championship begins. If the points were not reset at the beginning of the Chase, that noneligible driver could potentially still catch the Chase contenders by winning, say, seven of the last ten races.

The regular series NASCAR points system is used for the rest of the season. The points readjustment was only to remove the top ten drivers from the rest of the field, making it impossible for anyone outside the top ten to win the championship. The driver with the most points at the end of the season wins the coveted NASCAR Nextel Cup championship title.

Racing for the Fun of It: Non-points Races

Each season the NASCAR Cup Series welcomes two very popular non-points races, the Budweiser Shootout and the Nextel All-Star Challenge, in which the big-name drivers are racing, but not for valuable NASCAR championship points. Both races are basically all-star events with no points but big purses (big paychecks), making for a "race or bust" attitude.

The Nextel All-Star Challenge

The Nextel All-Star Challenge, formerly known as the Winston, has a rich twenty-one-year history in NASCAR Cup Series racing. The annual all-star event was run for the first time at Lowe's Motor Speedway in 1985, with Darrell Waltrip being crowned the first winner of the prestigious event.

The event gave a new meaning to the phrase "One Hot Night" in 1992, when it was run under the lights for the first time. Davey Allison stole the show when he crashed at the finish line with Kyle Petty. Allison was determined the winner by NASCAR scoring but had to be removed from the car and airlifted to a nearby hospital. This is the only documented Victory Lane ceremony in which a team represented a driver in Victory Lane due to injuries the driver sustained at the time of a victory.

The Nextel All-Star Challenge is held under the lights each year at Lowe's Motor Speedway, usually during the week leading up to the Coca-Cola 600, which is held Memorial Day weekend.

Girlfriend to Girlfriend

Some of the best racing you will see is during the twenty-sixth race of the season, which is usually at Richmond under the lights. Not only is it night racing, but it's also the drivers' last chance to get into the championship run. Tempers are flared and hearts are broken!

Drivers Eligible

1. Any driver who wins a race in the first races of the same season leading up to the All-Star Challenge.

2. Any driver who wins in the full season prior to the event.*

3. Past champions of the NASCAR Nextel Cup Series.

4. Past winners of the All-Star Challenge.

5. The winner of the Nextel Open.†

6. Twenty drivers must be in the field to run the event. If twenty eligible drivers are not present, NASCAR and Nextel will add drivers from two years previous in order to make the full twenty-car field.

---

*If a driver leaves the team he or she wins with, the driver is still eligible to race in the event with his or her new team. The car owner from which the driver won is also eligible to place their new driver in the event.
†This is a shootout race run prior to the All-Star Challenge for drivers not otherwise eligible for the All-Star Challenge.

The format for the All-Star Challenge changes almost every year in hopes of keeping the energy and excitement in tune for the race. The winner of the race receives $1 million. Not a bad night's work!

Past winners of the All-Star Challenge include Dale Earnhardt Jr., Jeff Gordon, Jimmie Johnson, Matt Kenseth, Mark Martin, Ryan Newman, and Michael Waltrip. The drivers with the most wins are Dale Earnhardt Sr. and Jeff Gordon, both with three. Davey Allison is the only driver to win back-to-back races (1991 and 1992).

The Budweiser Shootout at Daytona

The invitation-only Shootout officially kicks off Daytona Speed Weeks each February as the all-star race is run the week prior to the Daytona 500. The first Shootout was held in 1979, with Buddy Baker as the winner.

The race has changed names a few times over the years. What was known from 1979 to 1997 as the Busch Clash adopted a new name in 1998, the Bud Shootout. Another name change came in 2001 when the event was named the Budweiser Shootout.

Like with many other races in the series, NASCAR decided in 2003 to run the Shootout under the lights. Dale Earnhardt Jr. won the coveted trophy.

Drivers Eligible

1. Drivers who earned a pole award (top qualifying spot) in the previous season.

2. Past champions of the Shootout.

Past winners include Dale Earnhardt Jr., Jeff Gordon, Dale Jarrett, and Tony Stewart. Dale Earnhardt Sr. holds the most wins, with six.

CHAPTER THREE

Buckle Up, Drivers, It's Time to Do Your Thing!

There is much more to racing than just climbing in the car on race day and dropping the pedal to the metal. NASCAR Nextel Cup racing is highly competitive, with each team always looking for an "edge up" on the next team.

Before They Get There . . . Test, Test, Test

One of the ways teams get the edge up is by test sessions. Test sessions are non-race, non-points-related time on different tracks to test engines, setups, handling, etc. Test sessions are very important to the teams, as this is where they get their on-the-job experience.

NASCAR is very specific about the allotted number of test sessions each team is allowed each race season. This "tight reins" approach is NASCAR's way of giving every team a fair shot on race day by limiting teams (regardless of their budget) to the same number of tests. A low-budget team would otherwise not be able to compete against high-budget teams that could afford more testing sessions to perfect their cars. Limitless testing could ultimately play out during the race as the teams with more test sessions would have an advantage over low-budget teams.

This year sheds a new light on NASCAR's testing policy. For the first time NASCAR set a specific test schedule for all teams at certain tracks on a specific date. Also new in 2006 is the tire leasing program, which instructs teams to lease their tires for the testing session from Goodyear Tire Company. The teams are not allowed to use their own tires. The leased tires are returned to the Goodyear representative at the conclusion of the test session.

Any team (including rookies) can test at non–Cup Series tracks unlimited times.

The most popular non-series tracks for testing are:

- Nashville Superspeedway
- Kentucky Speedway
- Hickory (North Carolina)
- Greenville-Pickens Speedway (South Carolina)

Qualifying Mayhem

The starting lineup (the order of the cars at the start of the race) is determined by time trials a day or two before the big event. Qualifying is usually run on Friday or Saturday, and the race is run on Sunday. Qualifying is basically a race against the clock. The race field—the cars that will compete in the race—is made up of a maximum of forty-three cars, but most races have more than forty-three cars attempting to qualify.

Not just anyone can attempt to qualify for a NASCAR-sanctioned event. NASCAR is very specific about who is approved and who is not. The decision is based on track experience and driver seat time. NASCAR has something of a ladder system that a driver must climb before he or she is allowed to qualify for, much less race in, a NASCAR event.

NASCAR uses a random draw for the qualifying order. Each team has a representative draw a number on the morning of qualifying to determine at what point the car will run its qualifying laps. The team representative pulls from the draw in the order of owner points. The higher the team owner is in points, the earlier he or she draws for qualifying. Once the qualifying order is set, the teams get ready. The order a team draws is particularly important when it comes to weather conditions. Many times, the later a driver qualifies the better, as the temperature cools off later in the day. The rule of thumb is: cooler temperatures, faster speeds.

Qualifying consists of one or two "hot laps" (timed laps), depending on the

Girlfriend to Girlfriend

Many test sessions are open to the public at no charge. Although there is not much action (especially in a private test), it is still an opportunity to see the cars on the tracks. Some drivers host an autograph time to meet with fans. The tracks usually post testing information on their Web sites.

track. Drivers are allowed one warm-up lap before the green flag is waved for their qualifying attempt. Once all drivers have completed their qualifying laps, the race field is set, starting with the quickest car and moving back through the field. If a driver qualifies fifteenth quickest, he or she will start fifteenth for the race.

The quickest car and driver wins the pole award, which is the pole position. The second quickest is the outside pole position. Together, the inside and outside pole make up the front row of the starting grid (or race lineup).

Even though sitting on the pole gives the driver bragging rights, few pole sitters actually win the race. Many drivers believe it is better to start in the second through tenth spots rather than up front. As they say, when you are up front there is only one way to go— back. While not starting on the pole seems to give something of an advantage, a bigger disadvantage is starting in the rear of the field. Less than 10 percent of races are won from the thirty-fifth to forty-third starting positions. The main reason is that the slower cars run in the back of the pack, which can cause more jumbling up and wrecks. The biggest concern when starting in the rear is staying out of trouble. Any driver will tell you that when he or she has to start in the rear, the main focus is to move through traffic carefully and FAST.

In 2005 NASCAR introduced a new system that guarantees certain drivers qualifying spots in the race field. This rule change was made to protect regular series drivers from not making the race field if the driver happens to run a bad qualifying time.

The new system ensures the top thirty-five ranked teams (by car owner points) a spot in the race, providing they make an attempt to qualify. Seven additional spots will go to the fastest cars not in the top thirty-five in car owner points. The final spot in the starting field may go to a past champion of the series, as long as the driver competed in the series the year prior to the current schedule. If this spot is not filled by a past champion, it will go to the next fastest qualifying car. Bottom line, the top thirty-five rule only guarantees a driver a spot in the race; the field is still set on speed. The quicker you are, the better your starting position.

One exception to the rules for qualifying is the Daytona 500, which determines the starting order with the running of the Gatorade Duals along with time trials. The Daytona 500 is the most prestigious race in which to win the pole position.

Girlfriend to Girlfriend

While "sitting on the pole" gives drivers bragging rights, women racers are not as impressed with that choice of words. Patty Moise, who raced on the Cup level in the 1980s, once said in a humorous tone, "I refuse to say I am sitting on the pole."

Did you know . . .

If two drivers are tied for the top qualifying spot, the tie is broken by owner points standing.

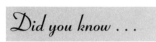

Did you know . . .

The Gatorade Duals race was known as the "Twins" until the name changed in 2005.

Drivers love the bragging rights as well as the media coverage that accompany the number one starting spot for the Super Bowl of stock car racing.

In the Daytona 500, the fastest qualifier from the time trials sits on the pole and the second fastest sits on the outside pole, making the front row of the 500 set in stone, regardless of the outcome of the Duals. The Gatorade Duals, run on the Thursday prior to the Daytona 500, determine the rest of the field for the great American race.

Slippery When Wet

NASCAR Cup Series race tires are not made for rain—period. The tires are slick, meaning they do not have treads (grooves) like those of passenger cars. Under normal race conditions, stock cars perform better with more rubber on the track. This creates better traction. There are a few tracks where rain tires have been tested, but they are not a normal factor on race day. For the most part, if it rains, no cars drive on the track, or at least not at race speeds. Why? Because it would be one slippery mess. The rain tires that have been tested do have treads (very much like a street tire), but they have not been proved to withstand race speed and forces.

Girlfriend to Girlfriend

NASCAR rules state that a race must reach the halfway point before a winner can be called. This basically means that once the race has run for at least half of the total number of laps, it can be shortened. NASCAR would rather run the full length of the race, but many races have been called after the halfway point because of rain or daylight issues.

If Mother Nature showers a track enough to cancel qualifying, the starting lineup is set by car owner points, meaning if you are first in car owner points then you will start the race in the first position and so on.

If it rains during a race, a NASCAR official will throw the caution or red flag until the track can be dried by turbo blowers. The cars will not be able to race at race speeds until the track has been deemed safe by NASCAR.

If a race is rained out, it is run on the next dry day, in most cases. NASCAR makes the final call on all rain issues. In some cases, NASCAR will reschedule a race to be run on another available race weekend, which happens very rarely. The series has competed on Easter, Mother's Day, and Thanksgiving weekends in the past because of weather or other unforeseen issues that kept the originally scheduled race from taking place or at least reaching the halfway point.

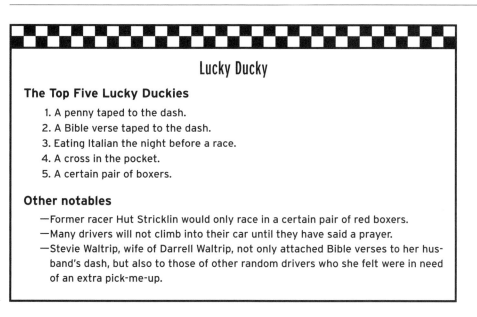

Lucky Ducky

The Top Five Lucky Duckies

1. A penny taped to the dash.
2. A Bible verse taped to the dash.
3. Eating Italian the night before a race.
4. A cross in the pocket.
5. A certain pair of boxers.

Other notables

—Former racer Hut Stricklin would only race in a certain pair of red boxers.

—Many drivers will not climb into their car until they have said a prayer.

—Stevie Waltrip, wife of Darrell Waltrip, not only attached Bible verses to her husband's dash, but also to those of other random drivers who she felt were in need of an extra pick-me-up.

Lockdown—The Impound Procedure

NASCAR introduced a new qualifying procedure in 2005 for certain tracks. In an effort to cut the escalating costs of Cup Series racing, the cars are impounded before twenty-one of the thirty-six regular series events. Once qualifying is complete, the top five cars in the field make their way to post-qualifying inspection to make sure all are "legal." NASCAR officials escort the rest of the cars directly to the garage area, where they are kept until race day. Once the top five cars pass post-qualifying inspection, they too are impounded. The teams are not allowed to work on their cars once they are impounded.

NASCAR has the right to make exceptions if special circumstances arise. EIRI (Except in rare instances) is commonly known in the garage area as NASCAR's blanket statement.

Girlfriend to Girlfriend

Most teams feel impounding is a ridiculous cost-reduction idea. The teams still have to report to the tracks on Friday as usual. They are not allowed to go home on impound days because of either cost reasons or travel time. The overall sense from drivers and crew members is that if they have to be there anyway, just let them work.

What's Happening on Race Day?

Let's face it, the racetrack is a driver's office. Being late for work (or in this case a race) would not be a good thing. But race morning schedules have certainly changed since the birth of the drivers' compound (which we'll discuss in chapter 5). One

Most Likely to Get Booed

1. Jeff Gordon
2. Kurt Busch
3. Tony Stewart
4. Robby Gordon
5. Kevin Harvick

of the reasons for the creation of this compound was so drivers could sleep later and get themselves to the track without the fear of being caught in race day traffic.

Most drivers get up rather early and eat a good breakfast. Some load up on carbs, while others choose to eat their carbs the night before the race. The quiet morning hours are spent in the motor coach with family. The drivers do not make their way to the garage area until midmorning, using this "calm before the storm" time to stay focused.

Each team usually holds a meeting by midmorning to review any race strategies or weather issues, concerns, etc. While the drivers and teams are gearing up, the cars are going through the pre-race inspection conducted by NASCAR.

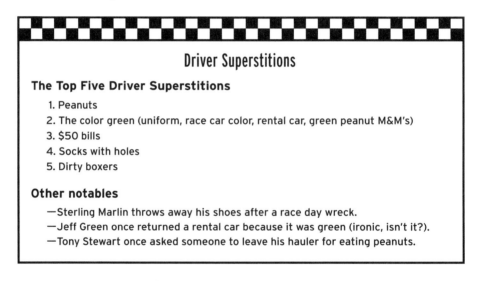

Driver Superstitions

The Top Five Driver Superstitions

1. Peanuts
2. The color green (uniform, race car color, rental car, green peanut M&M's)
3. $50 bills
4. Socks with holes
5. Dirty boxers

Other notables

—Sterling Marlin throws away his shoes after a race day wreck.
—Jeff Green once returned a rental car because it was green (ironic, isn't it?).
—Tony Stewart once asked someone to leave his hauler for eating peanuts.

Applause-Getters

1. Dale Earnhardt Jr.
2. Carl Edwards
3. Kasey Kahne
4. Jeff Gordon
5. Jimmie Johnson

A formal mandatory drivers' meeting hosted by NASCAR sets the stage for the race. If a driver is late or misses the drivers' meeting, the driver must start at the end of the starting lineup, regardless of where he or she qualified. The same holds true if a driver misses driver introductions. Mike Helton or John Darby normally calls the meeting to order. Mike or John will address concerns with drivers, discuss any rule changes, etc.

Immediately following the drivers' meeting is an interdenominational church service held in the drivers' lounge for drivers, family members, crew members, and NASCAR officials. This worship service is hosted by Motor Racing Outreach (MRO). Many of the drivers are very involved with the MRO services. Drivers like Dale Jarrett, Jeff Gordon, and Michael Waltrip have given their testimonials and led worship service.

Once the service is over, drivers usually head to the coaches or team trailers to eat a light lunch before changing into their uniforms. About thirty minutes before the start of the race, drivers must report to the makeshift stage on the frontstretch of the racetrack for driver introductions.

Drivers are introduced by their starting order (from last to first) in front of the main grandstand. This is where race fans have a chance to see their favorite driver. Many tracks also load the drivers into convertible cars and parade them around the track in order to give fans a better opportunity to see them. The same rule applies for driver intros at the drivers' meeting: if you miss it, you go directly to the end of the pack for the start of the race.

While all drivers agree it is best to get loud applause from the fans, some feel that getting booed is not so bad either. It is a common sentiment among the drivers that it is better to get booed than to receive no applause at all, which implies that no one even cares if they are there or not. Darrell Waltrip, past Cup champion and Fox race analyst, insists that "when you get booed, you know you have made it."

Once driver intros are complete, the drivers make their way to pit road. For most wives this is an intense time as they walk their spouse to the car. Even with all the fans and media members present, this is very much a private time drivers' wives have with their husbands.

Girlfriend to Girlfriend

It is not uncommon to see a driver be a fan favorite one week and in the doghouse the next. For example, if Jimmie Johnson wrecks Dale Jr. in the final laps of a race and the fans feel Jimmie was in the "wrong," Jimmie will most likely hear more boos than applause at the next weekend's race.

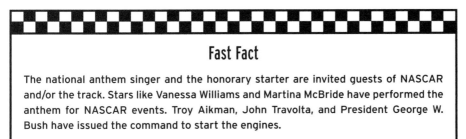

Fast Fact

The national anthem singer and the honorary starter are invited guests of NASCAR and/or the track. Stars like Vanessa Williams and Martina McBride have performed the anthem for NASCAR events. Troy Aikman, John Travolta, and President George W. Bush have issued the command to start the engines.

When the drivers get to their cars, MRO representatives are on hand to pray with them and their family members. This is a special time for many drivers, and

Girlfriend to Girlfriend

Many still remember the warm embrace the late Dale Earnhardt Sr. gave his wife, Teresa (on live TV), as they walked to his car for the start of the 2001 Daytona 500. Dale lost his life just a few hours later. There is always a feeling of "what could happen" when a wife watches her husband strap into his race car.

most will not climb in their car until they have made time for prayer. The national anthem is performed and the "Gentlemen, start your engines" command is spoken. Then the drivers drive off pit road and onto the track to line up for the start of the race.

Once the drivers fire their engines, everyone must clear pit road. (See more about pit road in chapter 7.) Crew members report to the pit stall as the drivers' wives either make their way to the pits or to their respective motor coaches.

When the checkered flag waves at the end of the race, the drivers hightail it to the airport, via escorted cars or helicopters. In many cases they are back home watching highlights of the race while fans are still sitting in race traffic.

CHAPTER FOUR

All Things NASCAR

There are more than twenty-five official sponsors of NASCAR, ranging from SunTrust Bank (the official bank of NASCAR) to Coca-Cola (the official soft drink of NASCAR). Most of these companies have enjoyed a long relationship with the sanctioning body. NASCAR also has many official suppliers who pay big bucks to be associated with the very successful top three stock car racing series. Nextel Communications Inc. is the title sponsor of the elite racing Nextel Cup Series, while Anheuser-Busch sponsors the second-tier Busch Series, and Craftsman Tools sponsors the popular Craftsman Truck Series.

NASCAR fans are the most brand-loyal of any sports fan base in the country. The official sponsors of NASCAR are willing to pay, in some cases, millions of dollars to be able to use the NASCAR name to market their products. There is no denying that when NASCAR drivers endorse a product, the product sells!

Sponsors, Sponsors, Sponsors

The business-minded people involved in and around NASCAR find a way to sponsor just about anything there is to sponsor, even if it means changing the name of a racetrack. The Charlotte Motor Speedway is now known as Lowe's Motor Speedway. You can bet Lowe's paid BIG bucks for that transaction.

Other companies find unique ways to market their brands in NASCAR. Goody's Headache Powders, for example, sponsors the "Goody's Headache Award," which goes to the driver who key media members feel had the worst day on the track.

The most important sponsors on race day are the main sponsors of each race team—what NASCAR refers to as primary sponsors. A **primary sponsor** is the "head honcho," the "bigwig," the "big cheese." It is what you see when you look at the race car, as its logo can be seen on the hood of the car and on the driver's uni-

form. Primary sponsorship in NASCAR Cup Series racing is quite expensive, averaging around $10 million a year, with top-level teams securing sponsorship for as much as $15 to $20 million. Keep in mind that whatever a company spends on sponsorship of a team can be almost doubled on promotions and the company involvement in a team. Dale Jr.'s face plastered all over your grocery store aisles does not come cheap. These are the hidden costs buried in not only sponsoring, but also promoting, a Cup-level team.

Primary sponsors get the most bang for their buck. Primary sponsorship dollars cover the majority of the race team's yearly expenses, but certainly not all; this is where the **associate sponsors** come in. These are companies that do not have as much money to spend for the sponsorship, but still will spend anywhere from half a million to five million dollars on a Cup-level team.

The Decal War—Why More Is Better

Have you ever wondered why in the world the race cars have so many decals on them? Most of the decals are so small you can't even read them. NASCAR racing is one of the most—if not *the* most—sponsor-driven sports.

Each decal placed on a car has to be approved by the team's car owner as well as NASCAR. NASCAR reserves the right to refuse any sponsor at any time. This is one of the many quirks NASCAR is allowed due to the fact that it is a privately owned company.

Most of the stickers/decals you see on the cars are from companies that have **contingency** awards for that particular race. A contingency award is a cash bonus award paid for by a certain company. In order to be eligible for the award, a driver must display the company's decal on his or her car. For example, a company can post a "leading at halfway" bonus, meaning that if you are leading the race at the halfway mark and you have the company's decal on your car, you win the cash bonus. The driver and car owner always have the last word on what contingency stickers and awards they will participate in. Richard Petty promised his mother early in his career that he would never allow beer decals on his car. To this day, if a Petty car wins the pole, the team is not eligible for the pole award money due to the fact that Petty Enterprises cars don't display beer decals. This also means that a Petty car cannot compete in the non-points Budweiser Shootout. (See more on the Budweiser Shootout on page 20.)

Other companies pay to have their decals on a particular car, just to have it on—with no strings attached. Race teams make a lot of money from companies who want their company "branded" with a certain team but aren't willing to pay the big dollars needed for primary sponsorship.

Driver Appearances

Both primary and associate sponsors are rewarded with a certain number of driver personal appearances each year. Obviously, the more money you provide the team, the more appearances the driver gives you. A young driver starting out can expect to make many personal appearances each year, sometimes more than what he or she is comfortable with.

The reason for appearances is to bring customers into the stores. In many cases the team and sponsor are attempting to build driver awareness with the fans. Rookie drivers are out and about in areas close to the track each weekend as sponsors and car owners try to build a large fan base for their driver. Bottom line: the more popular the driver, the more products they sell.

Girlfriend to Girlfriend

Drivers with more clout will have a lighter schedule of personal appearances. Dale Jr. and Jeff Gordon do very few personal appearances these days, and when they do they are very expensive. A company can expect to pay a driver such as Dale Jr. around $50,000 an hour plus travel expenses. That's a lot of Chevys.

Money Doesn't Grow on Trees

So where does all the money come from? The race purse—the amount of money paid out to the participants for each race event—is drawn from several different sources. The NASCAR participating tracks are required to pay for a portion of the winning purse. The tracks receive funding from four sources:

1. Race sponsor

2. Advertising

3. Ticket sales

4. Concessions

The top twenty-five drivers in final championship points also receive bonuses for their efforts. Funding for the points payout is made possible by Nextel (as the series sponsor), TV monies paid by the networks to NASCAR through TV rights

Girlfriend to Girlfriend

Winning drivers like Jeff Gordon, Kurt Busch, and Jimmie Johnson give a new meaning to the phrase "the rich get richer." Drivers of this caliber will almost always make more money on race day than their competitors.

agreements, and promoters in accordance with the agreement each promoter has with NASCAR.

Seventy-five percent of the posted race purse is paid after each event. The other posted monies are paid at the end of the season during the Nextel Cup Awards Banquet, which is held in New York each December.

Former champions and winning car owners are given the opportunity to participate in several different plans set up by NASCAR. For example, one plan guarantees a certain figure for participating teams for each race. This bonus plan accounts for why a driver not participating in the plan who finishes first may take home less than a participating team finishing twentieth.

The Giving Spirit: NASCAR Charities

NASCAR is a big business, but more importantly, a big family. NASCAR, along with the drivers, teams, car owners, tracks, and sponsors, takes the "giving back" attitude very seriously. Each year thousands of men, women, and children are impacted by the giving spirit of NASCAR and the individuals who make NASCAR what it is today.

Wish Fulfillment Organizations

The Make-A-Wish Foundation
www.wish.org

The Dream Foundation
www.dreamfoundation.org

Never Too Late
www.nevertoolate.org

Charities of NASCAR

Victory Junction Gang Camp—In memory of Adam Petty
www.victoryjunction.org

Speedway Children's Charities
www.speedwaycharities.org

The Women's Auxiliary of Motorsports, Inc.
www.waminc.org

Industry Organizations

The Dale Earnhardt Foundation
www.daleearnhardtinc.com

The Dale Jarrett Foundation
www.dalejarrettfoundation.org

The Green Foundation
www.jeffgreen.com/green_foundation.html

The Hendrick Marrow Program
www.hendrickmarrow.com

The Jeff Gordon Foundation
www.jeffgordonfoundation.org

The Kyle Petty Charity Rides
www.kylepettycharityride.com

Racing for Literacy
704-348-9600

Racing for a Reason
704-348-9600

Ricky Craven Snowmobile Ride for Charity
704-348-9600

The Ryan Newman Foundation
www.ryannewmanfoundation.org

Speediatrics
704-348-9600

The Tony Stewart Foundation
704-348-9600

The Ward Burton Wildlife Foundation
www.twbwf.org

Zippy's Crusade for Kids
www.gregzipadelli.com/crusadeforkids.asp

NASCAR Special Events

NASCAR Day
   www.NASCAR.com/NASCARDAY

NASCAR on Track for Charity
   704-348-9600

NASCAR.com Charity Auctions
   www.NASCAR.com

CHAPTER FIVE

Baby, You Can Drive My Car . . .

Becoming a NASCAR Cup Series driver is not an easy process. There really is no sure way of making it to the top other than racing your heart out every chance you get in hopes of one day catching the attention of a talent scout or Cup car owner. Every driver on the Cup circuit has a different story of their way to the top of the grind. Today's drivers face new challenges as well. Professional race car drivers from years past could make it to the top on skill alone; they didn't have to worry so much about marketability. Drivers on the Cup circuit these days not only have to be able to race at the top level, but also be articulate, well groomed, and maintain a high moral standard to the community.

It's a Family Tradition

Have you ever noticed how certain names seem to always be a part of the NASCAR race field? Have you noticed when reading bios of all the current drivers the many childhood and/or teen years a driver spent in his or her dad's race shop or working on an uncle's dirt car? There is a reason for that. Racing seems to be passed down from generation to generation. Could it possibly be hereditary?

Let's face it . . . kids of race car drivers grow up as "race brats," cleaning up around the shop, playing in the fields behind the shops; cars and racing become second nature. While some kids of drivers have no desire to race, it seems to be an

---

> ## The Difference Between a Race Car Driver and a Racer
>
> **Race car drivers** drive race cars.
> **True "racers"** know how to drive *and* build the car from the ground up.

Girlfriend
to Girlfriend

There are more race car drivers than racers competing at the Cup level, but a driver does not have to be a racer to be successful. There are many race car drivers who visit Victory Lane countless times. But the ultimate compliment was, is, and will always be the same: to be referred to as a racer.

early "need for speed" mentality that keeps many of them dreaming of climbing behind the wheel of a race car.

The names of drivers who make it to the top of the sport who did not grow up around racing can be counted on one hand; it just does not happen often. If your dad is a banker, chances are you won't be hanging out in a race garage or a short track, not unless he has his own need for speed at the local racetrack on Friday night.

Many would think a kid of a race car driver in the Cup Series would have racing opportunities handed to them on a silver tray. That would be the furthest thing from the truth. Most drivers (dads) find it imperative to teach their sons and daughters racing from the inside out, first showing them what's under the hood, then how to hit the accelerator. It is because of this approach that many drivers' kids grow up to be racers.

Brotherly Love

Another family tradition has carried on since NASCAR began—brothers racing against one another. In 1950, Tim Flock raced his two brothers, Bob and Fonty, and his sister Ethel, all at one time, making this race the only time four siblings have competed together in one race. To the shock of many, Ethel finished the race ahead of her brothers. The modern era has had its share of "brotherly love," with names like Wallace and Labonte leading the way.

Brotherly Love Notables
- 2004 Nextel Cup champion Kurt Busch and younger brother Kyle Busch
- Fox analyst and former Cup champion Darrell Waltrip and two-time Daytona 500 champion Michael Waltrip
- 1983 Winston Cup champion Bobby Allison and Donnie Allison

- 1989 Winston Cup champion Rusty Wallace and brothers Mike and Kenny
- Brothers Brett, Todd, and Geoff Bodine
- Elliott and Hermie Sadler
- Jeff and Ward Burton
- Jeff, David, and Mark Green
- 2000 Cup champion Bobby Labonte and two-time Cup champion Terry Labonte
- NBC analyst Benny Parsons and brother Phil Parsons

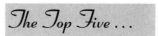

The Top Five . . .

Dream Dates

1. Dale Earnhardt Jr.
2. Kasey Kahne
3. Carl Edwards
4. Jamie McMurray
5. Jimmie Johnson

(Polled by 100 female NASCAR fans)

WAM, Inc.

The wives of the drivers also like to stay involved in this family-oriented sport. The Women's Auxiliary of Motorsports, Inc. (WAM, Inc.), strives to enrich the sport of NASCAR with a commitment to its families through fund-raising and wellness for those requiring medical or financial assistance. WAM also supports other charities with similar missions. The organization was established in 1965 as the Grand National Racing Wives Auxiliary; then the name was changed to the Winston Cup Racing Wives Auxiliary when Winston came on board as the title sponsor of the Cup series. In 2004, the Busch Series Ladies Association and the Truck Series Ladies joined forces with the Winston Cup Wives to form what we know today at WAM.

The Five Most Recognizable Family Names in NASCAR

- **France.** Bill France Sr.'s dream became a reality when stock car racing became more than just a weekend hobby for racers. France is the powerhouse family name in the sport. Most all the members of the France family have played some role in making NASCAR what it is today. With the third generation steering the way for NASCAR and International Speedway Corporation, the France family remains the first family of NASCAR.
- **Petty.** There should be no argument that the second family of NASCAR is the Petty family. Richard Petty has won more races than any other driver ever to race in NASCAR's elite series. The Petty name in NASCAR dates back to the 1940s, when Richard's father, Lee, was running the NASCAR circuit. Kyle, the third-generation driver and Richard's son, is a current Cup Series regular. Richard's wife of almost fifty years, Lynda, played a key role in changing the role drivers' wives played on race weekends. Lynda

has been an active member of the Racing Wives Auxiliary (now WAM, Inc.) since its inception in 1965.

- **Earnhardt.** Who can think of NASCAR and not think Earnhardt? The name means racer. Dale Earnhardt Sr. will go down in the history books as one of the most popular drivers of all time. "The Intimidator" got his nickname from intimidating his fellow competitors on and off the track, although his easy smile made you wonder where on earth that devilish nature came from. Ralph Earnhardt started the Earnhardt racing legacy over fifty years ago. Dale Earnhardt Jr. carries on the tradition as one of the most—if not *the* most—popular drivers on the current circuit.

- **Allison.** The name Allison stands the test of time. Bobby Allison was the leader of the famed "Alabama Gang," a group of racers that included his brother Donnie, Red Farmer, and Neil Bonnett. These racers from Alabama stole short-track wins all over the South, and local racers would alert competitors when the Alabama Gang was coming to town. Bobby Allison enjoyed an illustrious career until it was cut short by an accident in Pocono in June 1988. Bobby's wife, Judy, has been an active member of the Wives Auxiliary since 1965, and their sons, Clifford and Davey, both followed in their dad's footsteps. Clifford was tragically killed in a Busch Series practice session at Michigan International Speedway in August 1992, before he ever had the chance to race on the Cup level. Davey, however, was the sport's rising star in 1987. As the new leader of the Alabama Gang, he enjoyed success on the Cup circuit. His life was cut short in July 1993, when the helicopter he was piloting crashed at Talladega.

- **Waltrip.** Darrell Waltrip, dubbed "Jaws" many years ago by his fellow competitors, has been a driving force in NASCAR for over thirty years as both a NASCAR Cup champion and later a star Fox TV race day analyst. Darrell's younger brother Michael has enjoyed success on the circuit for many years as well, making the brothers very popular NASCAR personalities both on and off the track. When you think of Darrell and Michael you think . . . comedy. Both have a natural way with relating to fans at home, which is why Darrell is the fan pick for race day analyst. Darrell's wife, Stevie, has always been known as the redhead on pit road with the big smile. She is highly regarded by drivers' wives as a woman of wisdom. Michael's wife, Buffy, is very involved in the Motor Racing Outreach program.

The Top Five . . .

Hottest Hotties

1. Jimmie Johnson
2. Kasey Kahne
3. Dale Earnhardt Jr.
4. Casey Mears
5. Jeff Gordon

(Polled by 100 female NASCAR fans)

Home Away from Home—The Drivers' Compound

The NASCAR schedule is very hectic, making it difficult for the drivers and their families to spend much time at home; they live just as much at the racetrack as they do in their own houses. Pat Spencer, wife of NASCAR veteran Jimmy Spencer, once said, "I didn't know my neighbors at home but I knew everyone in the drivers' compound."

As the popularity of NASCAR increases every year, so do the number of tickets for each race, which produces heavy traffic flow. Higher ticket sales mean more people to get in and out of the tracks. While this is a very good thing for the sport, the amount of traffic is one of the biggest inconveniences for the drivers.

Rusty Wallace and the late Dale Earnhardt Sr. decided some fifteen years ago that the best accommodation for a driver is at the racetrack. Enter the drivers' compound. Every track on the NASCAR Cup circuit now offers a restricted area for the drivers' motor coaches, which allows the drivers and their families the convenience of staying trackside instead of in a different hotel every weekend. The interiors of the motor coaches are as plush as one can imagine. Remember, they are spending more time here than in their own homes. Many drivers will tell you they feel more at home in their coach than their primary residence. It is not uncommon to see big-screen televisions, gourmet kitchens, and bunk beds with individual televisions for the children or guests.

The drivers have full-time motor coach drivers who travel with the circuit across the country while the drivers fly or drive the day before the track opens. The coach driver loads the coach with the driver's personal items days before the trip. After reaching the race venue, he or she then makes a trip to the local supermarket to stock up on groceries for the driver and his family. Many coach drivers perform double duty as cook and coach driver, and some even have race day duties on the team. Drivers' families cook out together on the weekends, and wives

Girlfriend to Girlfriend

Drivers can't seem to get enough racing during the day. If you happen to walk around the drivers' compound area at night, you might see drivers sharing in friendly (most of the time) remote-controlled-car races. Tony Stewart has been known to burn the rubber off the wheels of his handheld race car. Drivers always keep score on their friendly Friday night feuds.

Fast Fact

The drivers' compound area is equipped with closed-circuit television that allows the drivers' wives and family members to know what is happening on the track at all times.

Girlfriend to Girlfriend

The child-care program for the drivers' kids is great for the wives, as it allows them the opportunity to go on pit road during the race or sit back in their coach with other drivers' wives and watch the race. It is basically a traveling babysitting service that provides worship and entertainment for the kids and a break for Mom.

spend the day with other drivers' wives, very much like a neighborhood.

The drivers' children often travel the circuit with their parents, as more kids are homeschooled than in years past to allow the drivers' families more time together. Many of the tracks have installed play areas for the children, making the compound a kid-friendly environment. It is not uncommon to see a playground full of children while the race is going on.

MRO—Motor Racing Outreach

The Motor Racing Outreach ministry was formed in 1988 to serve as a traveling ministry for the Nextel Cup Series. MRO is a nonprofit organization that provides prayer services for the competitors and their families, team members, and NASCAR at the site of Nextel Cup events.

The MRO staff provides child-care programs for the drivers' children through Bible study and creative/play time. The children's ministry of MRO has a traveling motor coach that travels from track to track with a full-time staff of highly trained ministry leaders for the NASCAR community.

The MRO pastors make their way down pit road immediately following driver introductions, as most drivers request to have an MRO representative pray carside with them before the start of the race.

The Top Five . . .

You Would Most Want to Say "I Do" To

1. Dale Earnhardt Jr.
2. Kasey Kahne
3. Jimmie Johnson
4. Jeff Gordon
5. Carl Edwards

(Polled by 100 female NASCAR fans)

The Youth Movement

So why are the drivers so young these days compared to the more mature age of drivers breaking into the sport in years past? It all started with racing megastar Jeff Gordon.

In 1992, twenty-one-year-old Gordon burst onto the scene with the Hendrick Motorsports organization. Crew chief Ray Evernham and the young Gordon found instant chemistry on and off the track, which many feel contributed to Gordon's early success.

Before Jeff Gordon made his very first Cup start at Atlanta in November 1992, most car owners chose veteran drivers with more experience; they simply felt the young drivers were too much of a gamble. At the time it was conventional wisdom that most drivers hit their prime in their late thirties, whereas many today feel a driver's prime is closer to age thirty. As Jeff Gordon continued to win races, more car owners were catching the "Youth Movement" bug. This movement changed the face of NASCAR, placing Gordon in the eye of the storm.

Most top-level teams have now added development programs to their organizations in order to find the next young megatalent to introduce to the world of NASCAR; drivers as young as fifteen years old sign on to driver development deals, leaving many to wonder, how young is too young?

The Young Guns

If you have spent any time in front of your TV watching a race or have ever read anything about NASCAR, you have probably heard of a group of drivers referred to as the "Young Guns." These are a group of drivers under thirty who are setting the NASCAR world on fire with their hard-charging efforts to make a name for themselves in the sport's elite group of drivers.

The original Young Guns are:

- Kevin Harvick
- Jimmie Johnson
- Ryan Newman
- Dale Earnhardt Jr.
- Tony Stewart
- Greg Biffle
- Casey Mears
- Jamie McMurray

Each year brings another new class of Young Guns to the sport. Drivers like Carl Edwards, Brian Vickers, and Kyle Busch are now carrying on the tradition.

The Rookie Stripe

A "rookie" is a driver who is in his or her first full year of Cup competition. There are many adjustments and learning curves for rookies as they make their way around the tracks competing with drivers who have much more experience. Being a rookie on the NASCAR circuit carries extra burdens as drivers adjust to the demands of racing with the best race car drivers in the world.

The Top Five ...

Dreamy Kissers

1. Dale Earnhart Jr.
2. Jimmie Johnson
3. Kasey Kahne
4. Carl Edwards
5. Matt Kenseth

(Polled by 100 female NASCAR fans)

Girlfriend to Girlfriend

Keep your eyes on these up-and-coming Young Guns:

- J. J. Yeley
- Reed Sorenson
- Clint Bowyer
- Denny Hamlin
- Aaron Fike
- Paul Menard
- Justin Labonte
- Martin Truex Jr.
- David Stremme
- Jon Wood

The Top Five...

Most Likely to Make a Good Impression on Momma

1. Jimmie Johnson
2. Kasey Kahne
3. Jeff Gordon
4. Carl Edwards
5. Jeff Burton

(Polled by 100 female NASCAR fans)

Girlfriend to Girlfriend

Other terms used for rookies are "wet behind the ears" or "green," both referring to their inexperience.

NASCAR has certain ways to label the rookies as newcomers. The most obvious is the yellow stripe displayed on the rear bumper of the rookie's race car, warning the other drivers that a rookie is near (much like a "student driver" sign). Most rookie drivers don't mind the yellow stripe, though some feel it makes them an easy target to blame for race mishaps. It is a big deal to the rookie drivers at the end of their rookie season when they are permitted to remove the yellow stripe from their car, a ceremonial acknowledgment that they are no longer the new kid on the track.

Rookies have to attend a mandatory NASCAR rookie meeting thirty minutes before the first practice at each specific track. Chances are the rookie drivers are making their first appearance at several tracks in their first year of competition. During the mandatory meeting, NASCAR explains track specifics and answers any questions the rookies may have concerning the track, race rules, etc.

The Rookie Challenge

Each year a new group of rookies make their way to the NASCAR Nextel Cup Series. They have a challenge week in and week out to race well with all of their competitors, but they also have a race within the rookie class. The Rookie of the Year battle is a highly competitive challenge among the rookie drivers.

To be eligible for the Rookie Challenge, a driver must: (1) qualify for eight of the first twenty races of the race season; and (2) have raced in only seven or fewer events in the previous year to retain rookie status the following year.

The Rookie Challenge has its own points system in and of itself. The winner of the prestigious Rookie of the Year award is given a trophy and award money at the annual awards banquet in New York City every December.

Many well-known successful drivers have won the coveted trophy and rookie honors in years past. Some of the past winners include:

- Richard Petty
- Ricky Rudd
- Jeff Gordon
- Dale Earnhardt Sr.
- Sterling Marlin
- Rusty Wallace
- Davey Allison

- Tony Stewart
- Kevin Harvick
- Matt Kenseth
- Ryan Newman
- Jamie McMurray
- Kasey Kahne

The Changing of the Guard

While there are many Young Guns just starting out in NASCAR Cup racing, many of the veteran drivers are winding down their careers, bringing about the beginning stages of the "new" NASCAR.

The hectic and demanding schedule of the Cup Series is at the center of the decision for most veteran drivers to hang up their helmets. Many feel their opportunities for top-notch equipment are getting tougher with the Young Guns moving onto the scene, which makes it harder for the veterans to race competitively.

Veteran racers Mark Martin and Rusty Wallace announced retirement plans in 2004, indicating they would either be running a limited Cup schedule or retiring completely from Cup competition beginning in 2006. Former NASCAR Cup Series champions Bill Elliott and Terry Labonte are currently running limited schedules in the Cup Series.

Some of the sports' biggest names are in the final years of their careers, leaving many fans scurrying to find a new driver to watch. Drivers like Mark Martin and Kenny Schrader have flirted with the idea of racing in the Craftsman Truck Series (nicknamed the "Senior Tour") once they retire from the demanding Cup Series.

Over the course of the next five years all of the following forty-something drivers will be faced with the tough decision of when to climb out of the driver's seat:

The Top Five ...

Most Likely to Make Daddy Get the Rifle

1. Dale Earnhardt Jr.
2. Tony Stewart
3. Kevin Harvick
4. Rusty Wallace
5. Robby Gordon

(Polled by 100 female NASCAR fans)

Girlfriend to Girlfriend

Many up-and-coming drivers will attempt to qualify and compete in a few Cup races in a season or two before advancing to their Cup Series. This is done to give the young drivers experience on the tracks before they make the Cup transition. The seven-race rule is in hopes of keeping the rookie field a fair game.

- Kyle Petty
- Ricky Rudd
- Dale Jarrett
- Sterling Marlin

- Terry Labonte*
- Kenny Schrader
- Bill Elliott*

The Legends Live On

While many fans mourn the loss of their favorite veteran drivers when they choose the road of retirement over the hard-paced Nextel Cup Series racing, such changing of the guard has been a part of NASCAR racing since the early years. Hundreds of drivers have come and gone in NASCAR competition, but only an elite few will be remembered as true champions. Hats off to the drivers who made the sport what it is today. These racers will always be remembered in the hearts of many as the true legends of the sport.

Bobby Allison
- The leader of the famed Alabama Gang and father of racing superstar Davey Allison
- 84 wins
- 57 poles
- Career winnings: $7,102,233

Buck Baker
- Died in April 2002
- Father of racing sensation Buddy Baker
- 46 wins
- 44 poles
- Career winnings: $325,570

Dale Earnhardt Sr.
- Died in February 2001
- Nicknamed "the Intimidator"
- 76 wins
- 22 poles
- Career winnings: $41,742,384

*Currently running a limited schedule.

Tim Flock

- Died in March 1998
- 40 wins
- 39 poles
- Career winnings: $103,515

Ned Jarrett

- Father of NASCAR great Dale Jarrett
- Affectionately known as "Gentleman Ned" by his competitors
- 50 wins
- 35 poles
- Career winnings: $289,146

Junior Johnson

- Became a legendary car owner after his driving career
- Served prison time for running moonshine
- 50 wins
- 47 poles
- Career winnings: $275,910

Benny Parsons

- NBC and TNT race day color analyst
- Affectionately known as "BP"
- 21 wins
- 20 poles
- Career winnings: $3,926,539

David Pearson

- Otherwise known as "the Silver Fox"
- 105 wins
- 113 poles
- Career winnings: $2,482,596

Lee Petty

- Died in April 2000
- Father of the King of stock car racing, Richard Petty
- 54 wins

- 18 poles
- Career winnings: $209,780

Richard Petty

- The winningest driver in the history of NASCAR
- Known simply as "the King"
- 200 wins
- 127 poles
- Career winnings: $7,755,409

Darrell Waltrip

- Fox race day color analyst
- Nicknamed "Jaws" during his career but now known affectionately as "DW"
- 84 wins (tied with Bobby Allison on all-time win list)
- 59 poles
- Career winnings: $19,416,618

Cale Yarborough

- 83 wins
- 70 poles
- Career winnings: $5,003,616

CHAPTER SIX

Where Are the Ladies? The History Makers

Women racers and NASCAR have had an on-again, off-again re-lationship through the years. Sara Christian, the first female to ever start a NASCAR race, made her historic debut on June 19, 1949, at the Fairgrounds Speedway in Charlotte. She finished a respectable fourteenth in this groundbreaking race, but her career never reached the level she had hoped for.

Janet Guthrie burst onto the NASCAR scene in the mid-1970s, hoping to be the woman to bust down the barriers against women in racing. She made history in February 1977 as the first woman to qualify for the Daytona 500. She started thirty-ninth and finished an impressive twelfth.

Patty Moise, Shawna Robinson, Fifi Scott, Louise Smith, and Ethel Mobley are just a few of the female drivers who have fought hard to make it in the male-dominated sport, but none have reached the pinnacle.

To date, no female racer has ever won a NASCAR Cup Series event; fewer than twenty have even had the chance to see the check-ered flag from a distance. Currently there are no female drivers rac-ing in NASCAR's elite series; however, it is not uncommon to find drivers of the female gender racing in NASCAR's Busch and Truck series.

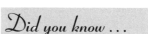

Did you know . . .

Until the mid-1970s, NASCAR made it clear that women (including drivers' wives) were not permitted to enter the pits.

The Pioneers

Driver	Years of competition	Number of events
Sara Christian	1949–50	7
Louise Smith	1949–50	11
Ethel Mobley	1949	2
Ann Bunselmeyer	1950	1
Ann Chester	1950	2
Marian Pagan	1954	1
Fifi Scott	1955	2
Goldie Parsons	1965	1
Christine Beckers	1977	1
Janet Guthrie	1976–80	33
Lella Lombardi	1977	1
Robin McCall (Mrs. Wally Dallenbach)	1982	2
Patty Moise	1987–89	5
Shawna Robinson	2001–02	8

Girlfriend to Girlfriend

Very few female racers have made enough money from racing to make the full-time transition. Shawna Robinson, for example, is a highly sought-after painter and artist, painting many homes of current Cup drivers and team members. She is also the mother of two children.

Female Racers—The Myth Uncovered (from a Woman's Point of View)

So why is it that female race car drivers have not been successful in NASCAR's top series? It's simple—equipment and opportunities! Ask any female driver and you will get the same answers . . .

- Women have not been given the same opportunities as male drivers.
- The best equipment goes to the male drivers.
- Few sponsors want to risk the hardships that female drivers face in the sport; sponsors want a sure thing.

Many wonder if it is possible for the male drivers to respect the female drivers.

Most female drivers will tell you they are respected, BUT most feel they have to work harder to gain the respect of their fellow racers.

Female racers have had to shrug off the age-old argument that women lack the physical strength and stamina of men. Many believe the female racer cannot "keep up" with drivers of the opposite sex. Others feel that "maternal instincts" in females keep them from driving on the edge, taking the risks the male drivers take in order to be competitive and win races.

Still others believe that female racers have not been given a fair shot at NASCAR racing, but things are changing. The NASCAR diversity program, formed in 2000, is ready to help stamp out the crazy notion that women can't win in NASCAR.

The Best Is Yet to Come—NASCAR's Diversity

When Brian France took control of NASCAR in 2003, he made it clear that NASCAR's Diversity program was of the utmost importance. Brian gave the Diversity program a shot in the arm when he handpicked his team to charge full speed ahead with the announcement in 2004 of an executive committee for Diversity, co-chaired by NBA All-Star Magic Johnson and NASCAR COO George Pyne. Tish Sheets, NASCAR's director of special events, took the leading-lady role as director of diversity, putting the program on the right track.

On Track

The **on-track initiative** program seeks to put minority drivers behind the wheels of race cars as well as securely place minority crew members on race teams.

- **Drive for Diversity.** Established in 2004, this program seeks to develop diverse and female drivers in NASCAR series racing events.
- **Joe Gibbs/Reggie White Driver Development Program.** Joe Gibbs and NFL Hall of Famer Reggie White partnered up with this program to help identify and establish minorities who have a desire to break into the world of NASCAR. Reggie White, who died unexpectedly in 2004, will be remembered in auto racing for his contribution to the growth of the sport.

Fast Fact

Drivers Allison Duncan, Terri Williams, and Sarah Fisher are involved in the Drive for Diversity program.

Off Track

The **off-track initiative** program seeks to create jobs and business opportunities for minorities.

- **Internship programs.** The summer internship program kicked off in 2004, placing some thirty interns throughout the world of NASCAR.
- **Urban Youth Racing School.** NASCAR's involvement with the nonprofit Urban Youth Racing School began in 2004. The Philadelphia-based school provides the opportunity for kids ages eight to eighteen to learn about motor sports.
- **Supplier Program.** This program supports and helps bring awareness of NASCAR to minority products in hopes of bringing the products to NASCAR.
- **NASCAR College Tour.** NASCAR and Coca-Cola have teamed up to bring awareness of the motorsports industry to historically black colleges and universities and Hispanic institutions.
- **Scholarships.** NASCAR supports and provides scholarships to historically black and Hispanic institutions in hopes of finding new talent and building awareness in the motorsports arena.

You might be a female NASCAR fan if . . .

You talk NASCAR with the grease monkey at your local auto repair shop . . . and you know more than he does.

Daddy, I Want to Be a Race Car Driver . . . Pass the Wrench!

While it seems unusual to some that a young girl would want to grow up to drive race cars, it is not as uncommon as you might think. An estimated five hundred young girls under the age of eighteen race in different series around the country. It is only a matter of time before one of these young ladies will capture a long-awaited win in NASCAR's elite series and *finally* put to rest the age-old myth that women can't drive race cars.

Fast Fact

NASCAR made history in March 2005 by running a regular-season Busch Series event in Mexico City.

Former Cup champion and Fox analyst Darrell Waltrip once said how exhilarating it was "to think of the number of young girls who are out there racing on local tracks that we don't even know about yet."

Move Over, Boys, It's Ladies' Night!

These are some of the female-driver movers and shakers . . . Take note!

Erin Crocker. Under contract with Evernham Motorsports to run limited Busch and ARCA (Automobile Racing Club of America) Series events, Erin caught the attention of many when she snatched the pole position for the March 2005 ARCA Series event at Nashville Superspeedway.

Kim Crosby. Running a part-time Busch Series schedule with GIC Racing, Kim is a former junior high school principal.

Allison Duncan. Under contract with RCR, Allison is currently running Late Models in Hickory, North Carolina.

Sarah Fisher. The former Indy Racing League driver is under contract with RCR. She is currently running the NASCAR West Series schedule.

Tina Gordon. Not currently with a full-time sponsor or team, Tina attempts to qualify for a handful of Truck Series events a year.

Teri MacDonald. Teri plans to run a limited Busch and Truck schedule.

Shawna Robinson. Shawna has run on and off in NASCAR's Busch Series, but is currently without a full-time team and sponsor.

Kelly Sutton. Kelly is currently running the full-time Truck Series for Sutton Motorsports.

Terri Williams. Terri is currently running in the Dodge Weekly Series.

Girlfriend to Girlfriend

Kelly Sutton has used her own battle with multiple sclerosis to promote awareness of the disease. Her brave attempt has earned the respect of many NASCAR fans and competitors.

Playtex, L'Oreal, Pampers . . . Oh Boy!

Just think for a minute the number of sponsors that would love to get in front of 75 million race fans each year . . . and 40 percent of them women. Are you kidding me? Calgon, take me away!

How much fun would it be to see a Playtex tampons car on the racetrack racing right next to the Viagra car? How about the Pampers entry taking the lead from the Jack Daniel's car? Nice!

Can't you hear the announcers calling the final lap of the Daytona 500?

. . . and coming out of Turn 2 they're three wide as the number 00 Hanes panty hose Dodge bumps the number 8 Budweiser Chevy as they pass the leader number 24 DuPont Chevrolet out of Turn 3 heading down to the checkered flag . . . Out of nowhere, the Pampers Ford wins the Daytona 500!

You might be a female NASCAR fan if . . .

You teach your children to count by NASCAR car numbers.

Let's just say the "untapped" female sponsor base would open a whole new world to the face of NASCAR. Between the ever-growing number of female racers, the fan loyalty statistics, and the female fan base, we might not have to wait too long to see more female branding in the male-dominated marketing arena of NASCAR.

CHAPTER SEVEN

Race Strategy

Racing is not just about who has the fastest car. In fact, in many cases, the fastest car doesn't win the race. A winning car is all about equipment, driver ability, strategy, a little luck, and a whole lot of team playing. Racing is a team sport. It takes the entire crew to pull off a win on any given race day. You can have the best driver and the best equipment possible, but if a team has a bad pit stop, its chances of winning quickly diminish.

Who's the Boss—The Chain of Command

As I am sure you have already figured out, race day is more complex than what meets the eye. While the driver is important to the team's success, it is the behind-the-scenes decision makers who determine who will do what and when.

The Top Five . . .

Most Recognizable Car Owners

1. Rick Hendrick
2. Jack Roush
3. Richard Childress
4. Ray Evernham
5. Dale Earnhardt Incorporated (DEI)

Owner. The Boss . . . the one and only "big guy." The owner makes the final decision on everything to do with the race team. Owners are too busy to make all of the decisions, so they hire people they trust to make some of the decisions for them.

Driver. The one who drives the car. The driver is handpicked, hired, and fired by the car owner. The driver is a big part of the race team, obviously, and answers only to the big guy.

Crew chief. Oversees all the race day operations, from what's happening in the race shop to calls made on the racetrack. The crew chief is the second in command at the racetrack, answering only to the car owner. The crew chief makes many decisions, from car setups to car changes, and is responsible for making sure the team and driver are all on the same page.

Team manager. An extra set of eyes for the car owner, more in the race shop than at the racetrack (that is more for the crew chief). The team manager basically "holds down the fort" by handling details like hotel accommodations, test schedules, ordering equipment, and hiring and firing.

Car chief. This is a newer title on the race team. The racing business has become so large that teams felt the need to split the duties of what used to be all on the shoulders of the crew chief. The car chief deals more directly with the team members to make sure they are following through with the commands of the crew chief, basically implementing the crew chief's plan of action.

Crew members. A combination of the over-the-wall guys and regular crew members. It takes many crew members to get the job done. Every crew member has an important role to play in the team's overall effort.

Other Team Members

Team scorer. Every team must have their own scorer to keep track of laps and times.

Spotter. Every team has a spotter who serves as an extra set of eyes for the driver. The road course tracks call for teams to use more than one spotter due to the layout of the course. The spotter communicates with his driver by radio. The spotter and the crew chief talk to the driver more than anyone else during the race. Spotters are usually located high above the track on the top level of grandstands or secured media levels.

Engine specialist. The engine specialist takes care of the engines at the tracks.

Tire specialist. The tire specialist takes care of the tires at the track by keeping up with temperature issues, tire pressure, etc.

Engineers. High-budget teams use engineers to find ways to make the cars better and faster.

Mechanics. The mechanics do a little bit of everything, from repairing damaged sheet metal after a race to making setup changes on the car. These are the guys who put the crew chief's calls into action.

Truck driver. Every team must have a truck driver to haul the race rig to the events. Many truck drivers also serve as team chef. You can walk through the garage area on race day and see truck drivers serving up burgers off the grill to the team members.

That, My Friend, Is One Big Paycheck: Who Gets What?

Race payouts these days are in no way, shape, or form comparable to race purses from years past. NASCAR racing is a big-money business. The drivers today stand to make more in one race than drivers years ago made in their entire careers.

To put things in perspective, Richard Petty has won two hundred races, more than any other driver in the Cup Series, a record that will almost certainly stand the test of time. The late Dale Earnhardt won seventy-six races in his career. Richard Petty's career winnings total just over $7 million, while Earnhardt's winnings exceed the $41 million mark.

That is one big paycheck, *but* the posted award money is a bit deceiving. In most cases, the award money listed is not what the driver takes home. The winnings do go to the driver (NASCAR rule 16-1), but the driver then has to pay the car owner his or her percentage as set forth in their agreement. The car owner then distributes money to other parties, such as key crew members. Each driver has a contract with their car owner that determines what percentage of the winnings they are entitled to, depending on the clout a driver has. A young driver starting out will get much less of the winnings than a seasoned veteran like Jeff Burton.

Girlfriend to Girlfriend

The driver's share of the winnings is the make-or-break point for many contract negotiations, especially with successful, highly sought-after drivers. It is customary for star drivers to ask for at least half of the race winnings. Young, inexperienced drivers customarily receive around 15 to 25 percent of the winnings, with added bonuses as incentives.

The drivers also receive a base salary, a guaranteed amount paid to them each month by the car owner. A young, inexperienced driver, or even a driver with little winning success, customarily receives anywhere from $200,000 to $400,000 a year for his or her efforts. A winning driver or NASCAR Cup veteran can expect to receive anywhere from $500,000 a year to over $2 million. It is reported that some drivers receive as much as $3 million a year as their base salary.

Certain key team members, such as a high-profile crew chief, may have a portion of the winnings in their contract as well. It is customary for crew chiefs to have performance bonuses as incentives for their countless hours and hard work.

Hit the Brakes, It's Pit Stop Time!

A pit stop is when a car leaves the track and enters pit road, which is located conveniently near the race surface on the inside of the race loop so that cars can enter and exit easily during the race. Every race team has a designated pit stall where their cars are serviced during the race. The pit stall locations are selected by the teams based on the order in which they qualify. For example, if Dale Earnhart Jr. qualifies on the pole, he gets first choice on his pit stall. The second place qualifier choses next, and so on until the entire race field has a pit area assignment.

There are several reasons why a driver would need to have their car serviced. The most common would be low fuel and/or new tires. Cars also enter pit road for repairs after an accident. NASCAR is very specific in what repairs they allow crews to make on damaged race cars. If the repair work exceeds the amount of time NASCAR feels is appropriate, the cars must move behind the pit wall or to the garage area. For safety reasons, NASCAR feels it best not to have a buildup of cars and crew members working on pit road.

The crew members who perform pit stop duties on the cars are also known as the "over-the-wall guys," meaning they are the men and women who climb over the pit wall to service the car. The best teams service a car for a normal pit stop in about fifteen seconds; this includes changing all four tires, cleaning the windshield, minor chassis adjustments, and topping off the fuel. The over-the-wall crew makes this happen by PRACTICE, PRACTICE, PRACTICE. The teams actually have pit stop practices every day at their home-base race shop. Most teams also have pit stop coaches to better prepare the crew.

NASCAR allows only seven crew members over the wall during a pit stop:

1. Front tire changer
2. Rear tire changer
3. Front tire carrier
4. Rear tire carrier
5. Jackman
6. Gas man
7. Catch can man

The Over-the-Wall Gang

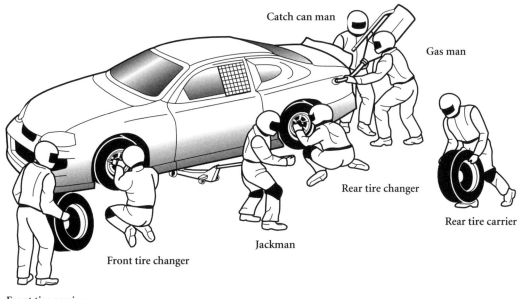

Catch can man

Gas man

Rear tire changer

Rear tire carrier

Jackman

Front tire changer

Front tire carrier

Pit road is one of the most dangerous places at a racetrack. NASCAR controls pit road speeds in hopes of keeping the race safer for drivers and crew members. The pit road speed limit varies and is determined by the size of the track, but is never over 55 mph. The pit road speed is announced to the drivers at the drivers' meeting prior to the start of the race. NASCAR-style cars do not have speedometers, so drivers use their tachometers to measure their speed. The tachometer gets a read on RPMs (revolutions per minute) of the engine, aiding drivers in monitoring engine power as well as gear selection. During the parade laps (laps run before the green flag waves for the start of the race) the pace car leads the drivers around the track at pit road speed so that they can get a solid read on their tachometer. The field of cars is split into two different groups (with a second pace car for the second group) during the pace laps to give the rear cars in the field a more accurate tachometer read.

Fast Fact

Speedometers are not used in NASCAR for two major reasons:

1. One more thing to break.
2. Tire changes could result in inaccurate readings on a speedometer; the tachometer, which measures engine speed, works just as well.

Pit Stop Strategy

Carefully planned and executed pit stops are critical for a successful race day. Many races are won and lost on pit road.

The Top Five Pit Stop Strategies

1. **When to pit.** Teams carefully plan when to come in for a pit stop. It is not uncommon to see a race leader come in for a stop and the rest of the field to roll in right behind him. The race off pit road is very important, as it sets up the track positioning of the cars.

2. **Fuel gambles.** Teams will map out their fuel plan before each race, but many things can happen during a race that can completely change the initial plan. The most successful teams learn how to go with the flow.

3. **Tires (two or four).** Tires wear out more quickly at certain tracks. It is a common dilemma whether to replace just two or all four tires on a pit stop toward the end of a race. Some track surfaces leave the teams no choice but to take four fresh tires, while other tracks lend themselves to only two fresh tires. Many drivers have won races by not taking the time to take four tires, getting them off pit road first and putting them in a higher track position than their competition. Another dilemma teams face is to use "sticker" tires (never before used) or "scuffs" (tires with a few laps), which can make a huge difference in on-track performance. Some cars perform better with scuffs, while others prefer stickers.

4. **Race traffic.** Race traffic is one of the nuances of racing. Not all drivers on the track are in race contention, making it bothersome for the leaders to work through the lapped cars. Experienced drivers feel that race traffic

can be used in their favor on race day if they are experienced in how to use the traffic as blocks and race support.

5. **Who's your buddy.** Drivers certainly have other drivers, be it teammates or friends, whom they seem to run well with during the race. Buddies can help block or open up places for each other on the track. The most frustrated drivers are those who do not have race buddies or those who feel their racing buddy didn't help them out. The most common tracks to hear of the buddy system are Daytona and Talladega. The term "drafting partner" is used quite often during these events.

The Draft

The draft is a stream of air shared in a line of close-running cars. It basically sucks the cars in, which seems to make them run faster together than they would apart. Drafting is employed primarily at Daytona and Talladega.

The draft is run single file with as many cars as can fit on a track. It can be run with two cars or forty-two cars. The problem with drafting is that if you leave the draft without a drafting partner you will be "hung out to dry" and lose the draft. It is not uncommon to see a driver try to make a pass (without a drafting partner) and quickly fall back to the end of the drafting line, which could mean going from second to fifteenth place in half a lap.

Few drivers have mastered drafting quite as well as the late great Dale Earnhardt. "Mr. Draft" kept fans on the edge of their seats waiting to see him pull off the "slingshot," a move that basically steals a little bit of the good air of the car the driver is attempting to pass. The driver attempting the slingshot must promptly turn their car to the right or left of their direct competitor and use the opposing car's air to pass with. This is a complicated move and one that few can pull off, particularly during restrictor-plate racing (discussed in chapter 8). The pride factor (or, rather, the fear of failing) keeps most drivers from even trying the slingshot.

The Top Five . . .

Most Notable Racing Buddies

1. Dale Earnhardt Jr.* and Michael Waltrip
2. Tony Stewart and Dale Earnhardt Jr.*
3. Jeff Gordon and Jimmie Johnson
4. Jamie McMurray and Rusty Wallace
5. Ryan Newman and Matt Kenseth

*Depends on which way the wind blows . . .

CHAPTER EIGHT

Hey, Baby, That Doesn't Look Like My Ford

The name (or idea) of "stock" cars came from the fact that racers used to drive their street cars right onto the track, run the race, and then drive home. The word "stock" referred to the fact that the cars were "in stock" at car factories. While the "stock" factor was indeed true many years ago, the stock cars used in the Cup Series these days are as different from a street car as football is from ice skating. If you dig deep enough, you might find a common screw or bolt that is used in both street cars and Cup cars, but that would be about it.

However, the ingenious phrase, "What wins on Sunday, sells on Monday," was and still is the idea behind most manufacturer marketing for stock car racing. Even though Cup Series cars are not anything like the street models available to the consumer, manufacturers bank on that age-old concept.

Fast Fact

The "stock" notion is a bit outdated, but don't look for the word to be dropped. It will likely never happen.

A Front-to-Back Stock Car

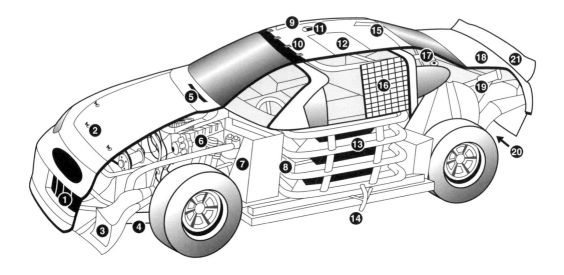

1. Front grille openings
2. Hood pins
3. Brake duct-forces
4. Anti-roll bar (or sway bar)
5. Cowl induction
6. Shock absorbers
7. Firewall

8. Impact data recorder
9. Roof strips
10. Windshield clips
11. TV camera
12. Alternate exit
13. Roll cage
14. Jack post

15. Roof flaps
16. Window net
17. Jacking bolt
18. Deck lid
19. Dry break fuel cell
20. Track bar
21. Rear spoiler

What Makes Them "Stock"?

The manufacturers involved in the elite series have changed over the years. The three current manufacturers of NASCAR stock cars are Ford, Chevrolet, and Dodge. Each has a certain style car they use for competition, though they change it from time to time. For example, Dodge changed from the Intrepid to the Charger in 2005. Any changes in body style must be approved by NASCAR, which can be a time-consuming ordeal. NASCAR is very strict with its car specifications in order to keep the playing field even.

Tire, Tire, Tire, Tire

Tires are a very big part of race day. A driver can dominate a race, come in for a final pit stop, take on a bad set of tires, and lose the race. The car "setup" plays a big part in how the tires perform on the track, as does the wear factor, meaning how

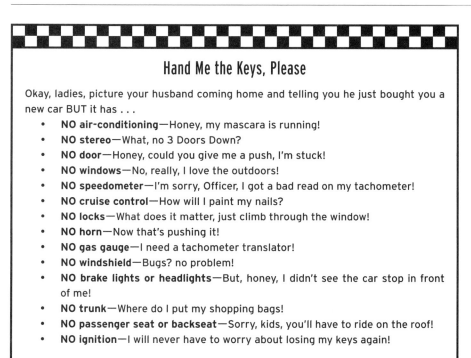

Hand Me the Keys, Please

Okay, ladies, picture your husband coming home and telling you he just bought you a new car BUT it has . . .

- **NO air-conditioning**—Honey, my mascara is running!
- **NO stereo**—What, no 3 Doors Down?
- **NO door**—Honey, could you give me a push, I'm stuck!
- **NO windows**—No, really, I love the outdoors!
- **NO speedometer**—I'm sorry, Officer, I got a bad read on my tachometer!
- **NO cruise control**—How will I paint my nails?
- **NO locks**—What does it matter, just climb through the window!
- **NO horn**—Now that's pushing it!
- **NO gas gauge**—I need a tachometer translator!
- **NO windshield**—Bugs? no problem!
- **NO brake lights or headlights**—But, honey, I didn't see the car stop in front of me!
- **NO trunk**—Where do I put my shopping bags!
- **NO passenger seat or backseat**—Sorry, kids, you'll have to ride on the roof!
- **NO ignition**—I will never have to worry about losing my keys again!

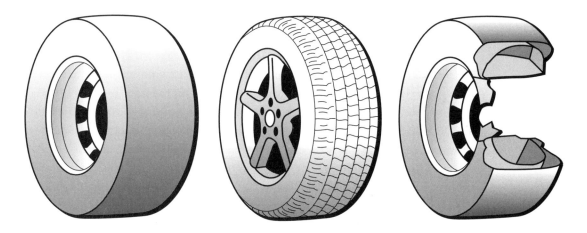

Left: a smooth tire—a race tire with no grooves or tread, which is why these tires do not perform well in rain. *Center:* grooved tire—a street model, just like what you would see on the interstate. *Right:* the inner liner—notice the inner liner inside the race tire.

long a set of tires will last. Some drivers are better at taking care of tires than others, and certain setups are easier on tires than others. While the tires are a very big part of a driver's success during a race, they are also a big part of the expenses for a race.

Cup Series teams will use between nine and fourteen sets of tires each weekend. Keep in mind that a set of race tires will run you around $400. In comparison, the average price of street tires is around $200.

In 1966, Goodyear introduced what we now refer to as the safety liner, which is basically a tire within the tire that enables the driver to recover safely from a blowout. Before the safety liner, drivers lost their lives due to violent crashes from blown tires. The inner liner has its own valve system, and can be used close to a dozen times if not damaged. The liner weighs in at 10 pounds and is inflated anywhere from 10 to 20 pounds higher than the race tire. The safety liners are used in all four tires at oval tracks one mile or more in length, with the exception of Bristol, which is a half-mile track. Bristol only uses liners in the right-side tires. This is due to the length of the track and the degree of banking. The energy (or force) at Bristol is all on the right-side tires making left-side liners a moot point. It would be very rare to have a left-side tire failure at Bristol, and if it did the banking would keep the car from pulling down the track.

Engines 101

NASCAR Cup Series race cars run with an eight-cylinder engine, which is the same size engine many street cars have under the hood. However, these high-powered specialty engines are built specifically for racing. NASCAR Cup Series teams spend thousands of dollars on engine development and the engine specialists who keep them running. Every successful team spends countless hours on finding an "edge" up on other engine departments. Obviously, the more successful your engines, the more speed your drivers find on the track.

Engines are quite expensive. A new one will set you back around $75,000 to $80,000. Some teams build their own engines, while others choose to lease them from other teams. A team can lease an engine for a discounted rate of up to $45,000. The key word here is "lease," which of course means the engine must be returned.

Engines need test runs just like the cars, but the teams cannot put an engine in a car every time the engine needs a test run. Engine builders rely heavily on the dynamometers (or simply "dynos") to test horsepower and engine wear and tear. The engines are connected to transponders that relay information to a computer.

On any given weekend, most fully funded teams will have several engines on hand in case of any unforeseen problems. If a team qualifies and happens to lose an engine before the start of the race, the engine may be changed. If this happens, the driver must move to the rear of the starting field for the start of the race. If a driver experiences a blown engine during the race, their day is done.

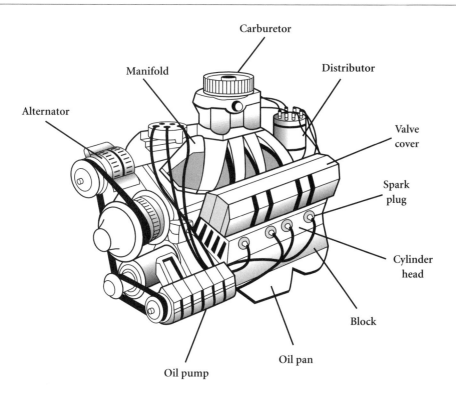

Carburetor

Manifold

Distributor

Alternator

Valve cover

Spark plug

Cylinder head

Block

Oil pan

Oil pump

Restrict What?

Restrictor-plate racing is one of the most controversial subjects in the sport of NASCAR racing. Before we get to why it is so controversial, let's talk about what a restrictor plate really is.

A restrictor plate is an aluminum plate that restricts the air flow from the carburetor to the engine, resulting in less horsepower and therefore less speed on the track. NASCAR distributes the plates to the teams on the weekends of restrictor-plate races. The teams are instructed to remove the restrictor plates each day after practice, qualifying, and at the conclusion of the race itself.

In 1987, Bobby Allison wrecked violently at Talladega Superspeedway. His car went crashing into the fence that separated the grandstands from the racetrack. Luckily no one (including Allison) was seriously injured, but NASCAR felt the wreck was a glimpse into what could happen. The next time the Cup cars made their

Girlfriend to Girlfriend

My best analogy for a restrictor plate is this: when you blow on a hot coal, it burns brighter. The same happens when you give more air to the carburetor and ultimately the engine—it runs faster. Restrict the amount of air and the car will have less power, less speed.

Girlfriend to Girlfriend

After Bobby Allison's scary wreck in the catch fence, several of the fans in the grandstands had to be treated for minor injuries, most for cuts and bruises. One gentleman refused medical assistance for a gash on his head for fear his name would be listed in the paper; he had told his wife he was working that day instead of going to the races.

way to Talladega, smaller carburetors were used while a restrictor plate was being developed that would pass NASCAR approval. By the time the cars made it to Daytona the following February, they were restrictor-plate bound. Currently, the only two tracks using restrictor plates are Talladega and Daytona.

So, why all the fuss over restrictor plates? Ironically enough, very few drivers like restrictor-plate racing, because they see it as dangerous. As the restrictor plates slow down the cars, the cars have a tendency to "bunch up" versus running farther apart. The drivers feel the reason for the bunching up is that cars are not able to pass due to less power under the hood. With cars running close together at high speeds, if one driver makes one very small mistake, the entire pack can be wiped out. Such a large pileup is referred to as "the Big One."

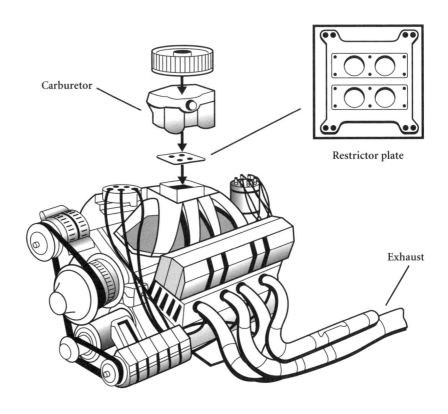

Carburetor

Restrictor plate

Exhaust

CHAPTER NINE

How Safe Can Racing Really Be?

Racing will always be dangerous—period! There is no way around it. If you race a car at an average of 190 mph with other cars running bumper to bumper, you know danger is near! That's why NASCAR has made safety a top priority. Since 1994, the sanctioning body has made more than fifty rule changes to better provide safe racing conditions for the drivers, crew members, and fans.

Safety in the Beginning

Safety has changed probably as much as anything in the sport. When NASCAR racing got under way in 1948 on the beaches of Daytona, the drivers wore blue jeans, T-shirts, and tennis shoes. Fonty Flock was famous for racing in his Bermuda shorts. Yes, they wore helmets, but not like the helmets we see today. The helmets were made of soft cushioned leather that barely covered the driver's head. Drivers wore goggles for eye protection and maybe an old pair of gloves. Certainly nothing like the getup the NASCAR drivers wear today.

The original idea of NASCAR was to be able to drive a street car right onto the track and then drive it home. In the early days, safety features in race cars were generally the same as what was found in a regular street car. Wanda Lund, the widow of Tiny Lund, once said, "The real men were the racers from years past. They didn't cry when they got hurt, they just kept racing."

In 1992 Davey's car violently flipped eleven times before landing on the hood. It was one of the scariest wrecks I have ever seen, but Davey's injuries were not life-threatening. Dale Earnhardt's wreck was calm and quick. There is an eerie feeling that comes over a track when tragedy strikes; it is there before any news is released. If you are around racing long enough, you know when a wreck is fatal. It's like a NASCAR sixth sense.

Unfortunately, it took the loss of lives to change many safety measures in the sport. Tires were to blame in the early years for track fatalities until the creation of inner liners. Fuel cells were introduced after the tragic death of Glenn "Fireball" Roberts in 1964. The HANS (Head And Neck Support) device was created and later made mandatory by NASCAR after the death of Dale Earnhardt Sr.

One of the many ways NASCAR plans to try and stay ahead of the safety curve is the Research and Development Center in North Carolina, which has many facets, one of the most important being safety. The center takes information from cars after accidents to try to determine better ways to ensure the safety of their drivers.

Who (or What) Rocked the Boat?

As with many things, it often takes someone or something to rock the boat before changes will be made. In February 2001, seven-time NASCAR Cup champion Dale Earnhardt was killed tragically on the last lap of the Daytona 500 in a wreck that most viewed as "not serious." Or so everybody thought . . .

The force at which Dale Earnhardt hit the wall was the worst type of hit a driver can take. A car that takes a direct hit and then tumbles or moves back down the track is far worse than a car that tumbles and then hits the wall. Think of it this way: if you throw a rubber ball at a wall, it comes back hard; but if the ball bounces, then hits the wall, it doesn't hit as hard because it absorbs a little of the energy with each bounce, rather than taking the full impact at once. With a race car, the idea is for the car (not the driver) to take the energy from the hit. When a car flips and tumbles, it is actually protecting the driver. Blunt, direct hits have nothing to absorb the energy—except the driver.

"We would not be remotely close to where we are in safety today if the icon of our sport had not been killed."

—Larry McReynolds, Fox analyst

The Wake-up Call

After the death of the Intimidator, Dale Earnhardt, NASCAR accelerated its safety efforts. The HANS device, impact-absorbing track walls, higher-standard seat belts, and full-face helmets are all safety areas that have become more advanced since Dale's death, and many of these are now mandatory safety features.

In 2000, Adam Petty and Kenny Irwin were tragically killed in separate accidents a few months apart, which coincidentally both occurred at New Hampshire International Speedway. The deaths of these two up-and-coming drivers shook NASCAR enough to start safety talks, but nothing gave the safety "wake-up call" like the death of Dale Earnhardt (who many believe was the best race car driver ever).

The Driver—Head to Toe

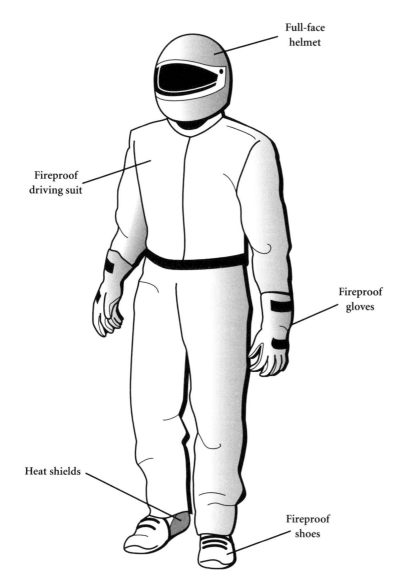

Full-face helmet

Fireproof driving suit

Fireproof gloves

Heat shields

Fireproof shoes

Helmet. In 2005 NASCAR made it mandatory for all drivers to wear full-face helmets. The open-face helmets from a few years back did not give the face enough protection from burns and other injuries. The full-face helmets make the drivers look like Martians but give the protection needed to the most vulnerable part of the body.

Uniform. The drivers' uniforms are made of a fire-retardant material called Nomex that protects the driver from fire and flying debris. The suits are very thick and hot, but a necessity.

Gloves. The gloves are also made of Nomex. The fire retardant gloves can either come right above the wristbone or go as high as a few inches below the elbow.

Shoes. Fire-retardant footwear is very important for drivers as burns on the feet are some of their most common complaints. While safety wear is often designed with accident protection in mind, the feet are subject to burns even without a wreck because the exhaust is right below the feet in the race car, sending out extreme temperatures. Not only do the drivers wear fire-retardant boots, they also wear an extra heat shield that straps onto their heels for extra protection from the hot temperatures sent out from the exhaust. The racing shoes look more like wrestling boots than shoes. The boot-style fire-retardant shoe laces up and ends right above the ankle.

HANS device. The Head And Neck Support device was developed to reduce the chance of injury caused by unrestrained movement of the head during a wreck (think whiplash at 190 mph). The collar-style device uses straps to connect to the helmet in order to keep the head from snapping forward during an accident. At the beginning of the 2002 season, NASCAR made it mandatory for all drivers in NASCAR's top three series to wear the HANS device.

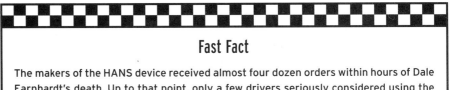

Fast Fact

The makers of the HANS device received almost four dozen orders within hours of Dale Earnhardt's death. Up to that point, only a few drivers seriously considered using the safety system. Many felt it was uncomfortable.

Safety restraints/seatbelts. The seat belts in a race car are balanced by a five-point harness system that basically uses two straps over the driver's shoulders, two straps wrap around the waist, and one between the legs. This system is very similar to that used in child safety seats or car seats.

The Cocoon—The Driver's Cockpit

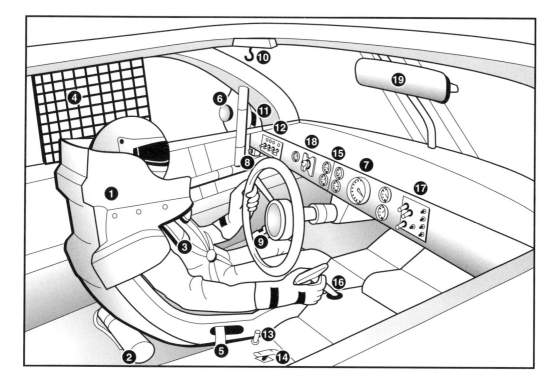

1. Safety seat
2. Fire extinguisher
3. HANS device
4. Window net
5. Seat-belt harness
6. Side rearview mirror
7. Tachometer

8. Ignition kill switch
9. Radio button
10. Helmet hook
11. Air vent
12. Main switch panel
13. Fire extinguisher
    discharge nozzle

14. Fire extinguisher switch
15. Engine gauge cluster
16. Gear shift
17. Auxiliary switches
18. Master switch
19. Rearview mirror

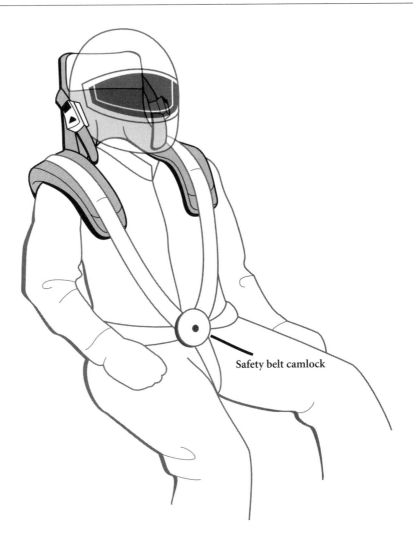

Safety belt camlock

Seat. Driver's seats come in many sizes and shapes. Most of the drivers use seats that wrap around the body like a cocoon. The wraparound seat helps protect the driver from injuries to the ribs, shoulders, etc.

Roll Cage. The "cage" is the steel tubing that protects the driver from rollovers. The roll cage is inside the driver's cockpit area and protects the driver from the outside. It is also the reason the doors on race cars don't open—a race car with opening doors would lessen the safety effectiveness of the roll cage.

The Car

Restrictor plates. The restrictor plate is a thin aluminum device that restricts the air flow from the carburetor to the engine, which ultimately slows down the car. Restrictor plates are currently used only at Daytona and Talladega.

Tire inner liners. The inner liners were designed to serve as a backup to a blown tire. In the early years of NASCAR, many severe injuries and deaths resulted from blown tires. The inner liner tire is not used on all tracks, only tracks one mile in length or longer. The inner liner is actually a smaller tire within the main tire.

Roof flaps. The roof flaps were designed to help keep the cars from going airborne. Ideally the flaps should open if a car lifts off the ground, basically serving as reverse wings to help keep the car grounded (like the flaps on airplane wings that slow planes down to land). Some cars still go airborne because they are simply moving too fast for the flaps to open.

Window nets. The window nets help keep the driver's arms and head safe inside the car. The window net is located where the driver's-door window would be.

Windshield. Windshields on stock cars are made of a plastic-type material called Lexan. Obviously, they could not be made of glass as this would be a huge safety hazard. The teams attach the windshield with an adhesive strip (sometimes several layers) so that during the race the crew can peel away a dirty windshield.

Fuel cell. The fuel cell (gas tank) in a race car is quite different from the fuel tanks found in street cars. It is located in the rear of the car and is attached by brackets to keep it from coming loose in an accident. The fuel cell is filled with foam, which helps to reduce the chance of explosion due to spilling fuel.

The Tracks

SAFER barrier. The SAFER (Steel And Foam Energy Reduction) barrier system is made of steel and foam affixed to the concrete walls of the racetracks. It was designed by Dr. Dean Sicking in order to provide an energy-absorbing wall to take some of the crash impact from the cars and, ultimately, the driver. As of 2005, all tracks on the NASCAR Cup Series circuit were equipped with the SAFER Barrier System.

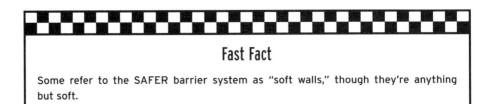

Fast Fact

Some refer to the SAFER barrier system as "soft walls," though they're anything but soft.

Did you know . . .

Another name for the free pass is the "Lucky Dog" pass.

Who Let the Dogs Out?

In 2003 NASCAR announced a rule change that forbids drivers from "racing back to the yellow" once a caution came out. The practice was used by drivers who were trying to advance positions on the track, or get a lap back if the driver was a lap down.

In most cases, the yellow caution was thrown due to a wreck. Drivers racing back put the stopped or slowed driver on the track in grave danger. After several close calls, NASCAR decided this age-old race strategy would have to stop. Not racing back to the line also allows the emergency vehicles to get to the crash scene quicker, as the race cannot be under green flag conditions when those vehicles are dispatched.

As a new twist, NASCAR introduced the "free pass," which is basically a lucky pass to the first driver a lap down to advance to the lead lap. This makes "racing back to yellow" a non-issue.

Forever Young

NASCAR racing has lost drivers in their prime for various reasons, but all tragically, leaving their names and accomplishments deep in the record books. These drivers made impressions in the eyes of many, impressions that will stand the test of time. One can only wonder what might have become of the record books if these drivers had been blessed with the gift of years.

Davey Allison

- Died July 13, 1993, at the age of thirty-two, after the helicopter he was piloting crashed into the infield of Talladega Superspeedway

- son of legendary racer Bobby Allison
- 19 wins
- 14 poles
- Career winnings: $6,726,974

Kenny Irwin

- Died July 7, 2000, at the age of thirty-one, from injuries sustained during an accident at New Hampshire International Speedway
- 1998 NASCAR Winston Cup Rookie of the Year
- 3 poles
- Career winnings: $4,606,943

Alan Kulwicki

- Died April 1, 2003, at the age of thirty-nine, when his plane crashed en route to a race at Bristol Motor Speedway
- 1992 Winston Cup champion
- 5 wins
- 24 poles
- Career Winnings: $5,059,052

DeWayne "Tiny" Lund

- Died August 17, 1975, at the age of thirty-nine, in a racing accident at Talladega Superspeedway
- Nicknamed "Tiny," though he was anything but at the imposing height of six foot five and weighing 250 pounds
- 5 wins
- 6 poles
- Career winnings: $185,703

Adam Petty (son of Kyle Petty and grandson of Richard Petty)

- Died May 12, 2000, at the age of nineteen, from injuries sustained in a racing accident at New Hampshire International Speedway

Tim Richmond

- Died August 13, 1989, at the age of thirty-four, from complications of AIDS
- Racing insiders referred to Tim as "Mr. Hollywood"

- 13 wins
- 14 poles
- Career winnings: $2,310,018

Glenn "Fireball" Roberts

- Died July 2, 1964, at the age of thirty-five, ironically from severe burns he received in a fiery crash in the World 600, thirty-nine days prior to his death
- Earned the nickname "Fireball" during his baseball pitching days in high school
- 33 wins
- 36 poles
- Career winnings: $290,309

Did you know . . .

Cindy Elliott, wife of Bill Elliott, was a full-time staff photographer for the *Winston Cup Scene* and *NASCAR Winston Cup Illustrated* magazines from 1989 until 1992.

Joe Weatherly

- Died January 19, 1964, at the age of forty-one, from a racing accident at Riverside, California
- Nicknamed "the Clown Prince of Racing"
- 1962 and 1963 Grand National champion
- 25 wins
- 18 poles
- Career winnings: $247,418

CHAPTER TEN

Rules, What Rules?

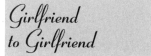

If there is one thing NASCAR has, it's rules. The official NASCAR rule book on any given year is about a hundred pages deep. At the beginning of each race season the sanctioning body establishes the rules by issuing everyone who has a NASCAR license or credential a new rule book. NASCAR goes to a lot of time and expense to make sure that everyone understands the rules.

While some drivers push the rule envelope (we will get to this later), NASCAR clearly (well, kind of) states what is legal and what is not. The organization has a full-time team of officials whose sole responsibility is to make sure the cars are legal and that teams are playing by the rules set before them.

Inspect This

Every race car you see on race day has to go through several inspections throughout the course of a race weekend. Two of the most thorough are the pre-race and post-race inspections. While all participating cars must pass through pre-race inspection, only the top five finishers are checked during post-race inspection.

Some of the areas NASCAR looks at for inspection violations are:

- Engine
- Fuel cell
- Sheet metal
- Safety equipment
- Body (car) dimensions
- Roll bar
- Tires

Girlfriend to Girlfriend

Most of the rules are in hopes of keeping cars safe and on a level playing field. NASCAR uses the rules to keep one team from running away with every race. How much fun would racing be if the same driver always won? Not much!

The "Gray Area"

As with any sport, it is important to remember who makes the rules and who calls the shots—NASCAR inspectors and officials (who by the way are HUMAN). Enter human error, a.k.a. the infamous "gray area."

The technical rules for pre-race and post-race inspection are less likely to lend themselves to the "gray area" debate. However, on-track rules and on-track penalties are free game for shots from drivers and fans accusing NASCAR of showing special treatment to certain drivers.

Many feel the heavily used NASCAR rule 12-4-A, "Actions Detrimental to Stock Car Racing," was established for nothing other than the "gray area." This rule has been used more than any other NASCAR rule, penalizing drivers for everything from using inappropriate language to using an "illegal" car part.

Fast Fact

Pit stop violations and on-track incidents are among the areas in which NASCAR hands down penalties after inspection.

Girlfriend to Girlfriend

NASCAR has been accused of many things, but being stupid is not one of them. Most rules set by NASCAR have a very small "out," which in this case is referred to as the "gray area." Hmm . . . it's all in the interpretation.

The Unspoken Rules— The "Gentleman's Agreement"

NASCAR drivers, as with most sports, have their own set of unwritten rules, referred to in NASCAR as the "gentleman's agreement." Drivers are much more likely to overlook a driver who violates a NASCAR rule than if a driver breaks the gentleman's code of ethics.

The code is based on how drivers treat other drivers on the track—simply put, driver's etiquette. If a driver is referred to as a "clean racer" then you know this is a driver who respects the boundaries of other cars and drivers on the track. "Clean racers" are drivers who race with integrity.

The Top Three Gentleman's Rules

1. If you are lapped traffic, move over to allow front-runners to get by. This is especially important in the last ten laps.

2. If you are a noncompetitive car or lapped traffic, do not do anything to affect the outcome of the race by blocking, challenging race leaders, etc.

3. Use good judgment as to when to "bump draft." Never bump draft in a turn; only use this technique when you are on the straightaway.

Girlfriend to Girlfriend

Contrary to what some drivers say, on-track conflicts do determine off-track relationships. If a driver continually denies the gentleman's agreement, he will not be treated with the same respect off the track as other drivers. The worst place a driver can be is on the outside looking in. NASCAR racing is a big business but a small *family*.

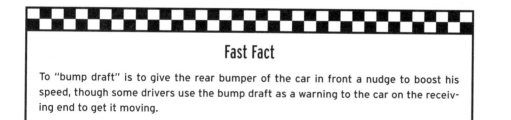

Fast Fact

To "bump draft" is to give the rear bumper of the car in front a nudge to boost his speed, though some drivers use the bump draft as a warning to the car on the receiving end to get it moving.

"Rough," "dirty," or "bully" racers are drivers who are not respected by their fellow competitors. This style driver is only concerned with winning a race and will do anything to get that win, even if it means racing outside the code of ethics.

Oops, You Mean I Can't Say That?

It's no secret that NASCAR has worked hard over the past five years to change its image in many eyes from a southern redneck sport to a highly regarded mainstream one. As the fan and media base of NASCAR continue to grow at a rapid pace, so does the scrutiny that goes along with its success.

NASCAR has made it clear to their drivers the importance of being respectful in interviews and the use of appropriate behavior at all times. NASCAR has also

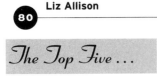

made it clear that any violation of this code of ethics will be dealt with accordingly . . . (enter gray area).

It was not too long ago when drivers would (and could) climb out of their cars and express how they felt about other drivers' actions on the track. Drivers are still allowed to do that BUT must "use words wisely," as NASCAR president Mike Helton continually reminds them. Helton addressed the inappropriate language issue in 2004 after several drivers were penalized for using inappropriate language during post-race interviews (most notably Dale Earnhardt Jr., who was fined $10,000 and 25 championship points) by stating that "if you wouldn't want your grandmother to hear it, don't say it."

NASCAR has been accused of making the driver interviews "boring" and "blah" by not allowing the drivers to openly communicate their feelings or frustration, while others feel NASCAR has made a respectable stand on maintaining a positive reflection for the fans, particularly the younger fans.

Girlfriend to Girlfriend

In their defense, the drivers have been cramped up in a race car for hours racing at speeds up to 200 mph. These are highly competitive drivers who have competed in what many times is an aggravated state, close racing, race traffic, car problems, etc. It would take a very mature, levelheaded person to climb out of the car, immediately have a microphone and "live" camera thrown in his face, and manage to watch his p's and q's. For some, this would be the toughest job of the day.

The Cheating Kind

"Being creative," "finding an edge," "gray area," and "rule interpretation" are all nice ways of saying someone CHEATED! So why would drivers risk cheating when NASCAR clearly states that "cheating will not be tolerated"? Many teams feel the answer is simply . . . why not?

The sponsorship dollars teams have at stake these days makes it tough for them not to look for an edge up on their competition, even if it does mean bending the rules a bit.

NASCAR now has very strict guidelines for their participating teams on how cheating will be dealt with. It has been just in the last few years that the organization has taken this strong stand on the age-old practice of cheating and racing. NASCAR's rule 12-4-Q clearly states that anyone whose car, car part, component, or equipment does not conform to NASCAR rules or has been altered to detract from or compromise the integrity of NASCAR racing will be penalized or suspended. If a team is found in violation of these rules, the common penalty is a $10,000 fine, 25 points deducted from driver points, and another 25 points deducted from car owner points, as well as a probationary period.

But, Your Honor, Please!

Like most mainstream sports, NASCAR has an appeals process for any violation handed down to car owners, drivers, or crew members. If a car owner, driver, or crew member feels they have been unfairly penalized, they may appeal to the National Stock Car Racing Commission within ten days of the date of the penalty notice. The commission will meet to hear the appeal and either drop the penalty, reduce the penalty, or uphold the penalty. If the penalty is upheld, a team or driver can appeal the appeal. In some rare instances, the penalties are actually increased after the commission hears the case.

The Flags

NASCAR flags are used for every NASCAR event. Each flag signifies something very important to the drivers. The NASCAR flagman is the same person week in and week out. The flagman only waves a flag when the designated NASCAR official (usually David Hoots) has made the determination of a potential problem or race issue. The flagman is the communication between NASCAR and the drivers during the race.

- **Green flag.** Green means GO GO GO, or, as Darrell Waltrip puts it, "Boogity Boogity Boogity."

- **Yellow flag.** Yellow means caution on the track. Once the caution flag is waved, the entire field of cars must slow down and line up in single file.

- **Red flag.** Red means stop! NASCAR will advise the drivers where they are to stop, which sometimes is a certain area of the track. Red flags are used for serious accidents, weather conditions, or lengthy cautions due to cleanup, etc.

- **Black flag.** If a driver is black-flagged he is being informed by NASCAR to leave the track immediately by entering his pits and by reporting to a NASCAR official. Reasons for this would be if a car is being penalized for a pit road speeding

"It's only cheating if you get caught . . . right?"

—Bobby Allison, 1983 Winston Cup champion

Girlfriend to Girlfriend

Okay, girls, the drivers care NOTHING about the monetary fine, trust me on this. But if you start taking the wins away from drivers or a larger points penalty, the teams will think twice before they go the cheating route. NASCAR has to make it NOT worth the gamble before teams seriously consider not stepping outside of the lines.

Girlfriend to Girlfriend

Many feel the NASCAR appeals process is often not worth the effort. Few appeals are overturned, a few are reduced, but most are upheld—period! "Appealing the appeal" would be even more frustrating. NASCAR hands down a penalty because they feel a team or driver is in the wrong. That judgment call is quite commonly questioned, but hardly ever overturned.

violation, other track violation, or not meeting the track's minimum race speed.

- **Black flag with white stripe.** This is used when a driver who was black-flagged chose not to report to the pits. This flag notifies the driver and team that they will no longer be scored by NASCAR, basically making their laps not count.

- **Blue flag with yellow stripe.** The blue flag is used quite often during the race. A driver who receives a wave of the blue flag is being advised to allow the lead cars or faster cars to pass. Drivers receiving this flag must yield to the faster cars.

- **White flag.** The white flag signals that the end of the race is near. This is the one-lap-to-go flag. All heck breaks loose when the white flag comes out. Basically, it's do-or-die time.

- **Checkered flag.** Awwww, the black-and-white checkered flag. This is the "big boy," the "Big Kahuna," the "granddaddy" of flags. The driver who is the first across the start/finish line and receives the waving of the checkered flag wins the race. Out of all the flags, this is the most sought after. Some drivers race their entire Cup careers without ever receiving the coveted checkered flag, while others make it look pretty darn easy.

CHAPTER ELEVEN

Celebration!

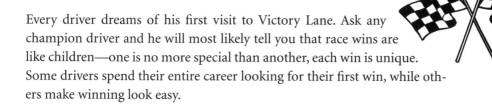

Every driver dreams of his first visit to Victory Lane. Ask any champion driver and he will most likely tell you that race wins are like children—one is no more special than another, each win is unique. Some drivers spend their entire career looking for their first win, while others make winning look easy.

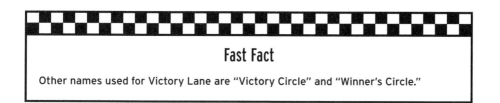

Fast Fact

Other names used for Victory Lane are "Victory Circle" and "Winner's Circle."

Victory Lane

Victory Lane is positioned in a different spot at each track. However, most are near the frontstretch where the festivities can be seen by the fans in the grandstands. Martinsville Speedway actually conducts the Victory Lane celebration on the racetrack, right in front of the main grandstands. This is a fan favorite track because of the accessibility of the drivers.

Victory Lane is not a road or a straight lane like the name leads you to believe. It is actually a fenced-in area or designated area that is more commonly in the shape of a circle, making the name "Victory Circle" more appropriate. The fenced-in area is usually surrounded by grass and shrubs, making a pleasant view for TV coverage and media opportunities.

Victory Lane Stories from NASCAR Wives

Liz Allison

I remember sitting in a van in the infield at Bristol Motor Speedway with Ann Schrader, wife of veteran Kenny Schrader, when I was a young driver's wife. The laps of the race were winding down, and Davey was in contention to win the race. The old infield at Bristol was surrounded by a twelve-foot chain-link fence. If you were deep in the drivers' parking area (which we were) there was no way to get to Victory Lane without walking (or running) all the way to the other end of the parking area and all the way back down the front pit road area. At a fast pace, it would still take a good seven to ten minutes. Understand that Victory Lane was in reaching distance from where we were parked but a BIG fence was between us. I refused to head to Victory Lane until Davey officially won the race for fear I would "jinx" the win. With that being said, I had to get to Victory Lane fast after he did, in fact, win. I decided to climb the fence instead of taking ten minutes to walk around. I made it up fine, but as I was climbing over to the other side, my sweater got caught on the wire sticking out at the top of the fence. It did not take me long to realize I WAS STUCK! As Davey climbed out of his car, photographers pointed at me (yes, his wife) sitting on top of the fence waiting for someone (anyone) to rescue me. A track official very nicely climbed to the top of the fence to help me down. After a few snips with the scissors I was free to go celebrate. Davey was not amused.

Girlfriend to Girlfriend

There are several beverages that are ceremonially "sprayed" in Victory Lane. Pepsi seems to have the highest cause for alarm as it apparently burns the eyes the most. You know those tears you think are coming from pride and joy? It's the Pepsi.

Burnout Baby

After the winning driver crosses the finish line, he takes a cool-down lap around the track to wave at the fans. Once the driver reaches the frontstretch area, he either does doughnuts or a burnout; some do both. A burnout is where the driver adjusts the brakes to stop the front wheels as the rear wheels are turning, creating lots of smoke. The (not so smoky) doughnut is where the driver basically turns the car in circles. It has become a competition of sorts to see which driver gives the best burnout. The better the burnout, the louder the crowd cheers.

A few drivers feel the burnout is too predictable and old-fashioned. Some actually refuse to give the fans the move, opting for the more laid-back approach . . . like the victory lap without the bells and whistles. *Come on boys, lighten up!*

Another victory lap ceremony is the "Polish victory lap," which is where the driver turns the car around and actually makes a lap going in the opposite

Fast Fact

Jimmie Johnson did such an eye-opening burnout at Fontana after his very first Cup career win in 2002 (his rookie season) that he actually blew up the engine.

direction. This places the driver's window closest to the fans, who love the better view of the driver. This was made famous by the late Alan Kulwicki in his short career, which spanned from the late eighties until his untimely death in April 1993, after his private airplane crashed en route to Bristol Motor Speedway.

One driver in particular has continued to make headlines with his trademark victory celebration. Carl Edwards does a (quite impressive) backflip when he wins a race, making him a fan favorite. Many fans and media members refer to Carl as "Flipper," after the fun-loving TV dolphin.

Once the burnouts/doughnuts/backflips (take your pick) are complete, the winning driver takes his car down pit road. As the driver passes, he or she shakes hands with crew members on the way to Victory Lane.

The Top Five ...

Burnouts

1. Kevin Harvick
2. Kurt Busch
3. Tony Stewart
4. Jeff Gordon
5. Jimmie Johnson

The Champions Trophy

The coveted NASCAR Nextel Cup Series trophy is awarded to the top-finishing driver each year at the annual awards banquet in New York City. Technically, the award is not a cup, which would seem illogical seeing that it is the Cup Series.

Trophy specifics:

Height: 24 inches
Weight: 27 pounds
Materials: Sterling silver and wood
Created by: Tiffany & Co.
Designed by: Bruce Newman
Production time: Four months

Victory Lane Stories from NASCAR Wives

Angie Skinner

Angie Skinner, wife of Mike Skinner, shocked the racing world when she showed her excitement after Mike won one of the Twins qualifying events for the Daytona 500. As Angie ran up to congratulate her husband, she jumped up in his arms, wrapped her legs around his waist, and landed the biggest smooch you have ever seen on his lips. Angie said this was her way of showing Mike her "you-are-awesome affection." The AP photo of her legs wrapped around Mike was the talk of the motorsports world for weeks thereafter. In February 2001, the late Dale Earnhardt Sr. walked up to Angie at drivers' introduction and whispered in her ear, "I like that photo of you with your legs all around Mike after the Twins win . . . you do that every time he wins, you hear me?" She assured him she would. To this day people ask Angie about her celebration with her husband after his Twins win. Her comment was and still is, "It's just something between us."

Who's Invited?

Victory Lane is a heavily secured area where the team celebrates with their driver. Family members, sponsor representatives, NASCAR officials, close friends, track representatives, manufacturer representatives, and NASCAR-approved media are the only people allowed in Victory Lane.

Security checks the credentials of every person attempting to enter the festivities. Even with the short list of approved guests, Victory Lane quickly becomes the biggest party in town. "Controlled chaos" is the most accurate description for the celebration.

Girlfriend to Girlfriend

I have heard stories of fans ever so cleverly slipping into Victory Lane unnoticed. I met a fan once who showed me where he was in official team pictures alongside the crew members giving the thumbs-up to the cameras. No one realized he was not supposed to be there.

Lights, Camera, Action!

The first thing a driver does when he gets to Victory Lane is . . . WAIT! Can you imagine—you just won a race and now you have to sit in your car and wait to get out? Enter "live" television.

NASCAR has an agreement with the networks that drivers will stay in their cars until they are signaled from the providing network to climb out of their car. Yes, that perfectly timed interview you see week in and week out is planned. Sorry!

There is a pecking order for the media that is made crystal clear to both competitors and media members that no one shall cross. It is as follows:

1. Providing network—live coverage

2. Providing radio—live coverage

3. Track PA and local media

4. NASCAR-approved media, including but not limited to the Speed Channel, ESPN, and Fox Sports

After the initial interviews are complete, the driver very briefly gets to kiss his spouse and shake hands with crew members before "the dance" begins . . .

The Hat Dance

As much as the drivers appreciate every single sponsor involved with their team and that specific race, the "hat dance" is the most grueling (and somewhat comical) part of the Victory Lane ceremonies.

Once the radio and television interviews are complete, the driver poses for pictures (hundreds) with sponsor representatives, which includes the driver wearing a ball cap with every sponsor's name or logo. Most drivers can expect at least twenty different hats to be planted on their heads.

An official hands the hat to the driver, the driver smiles for a picture, then throws the hat, the next hat is handed to the driver, and so on . . . You get the picture. The driver does this hat dance until every sponsor has had their Kodak moment.

Until the Midnight Hour

Once the driver has completed all of the Victory Lane pictures and interviews, he is snatched up by track officials and escorted to the press box for a question-and-answer session with *more* reporters.

We're not done yet . . . now it's time for the high-dollar suites. NASCAR and the hosting track have very special guests who are invited to attend races in the suites high above the grandstands. The driver tours the suites to welcome the VIPs, pose for *more* pictures, and sign a few *more* autographs before finally calling it a day. By the time the driver's winning duties have wrapped up, his team

Girlfriend to Girlfriend

The feel and tone of the post-race interview is in the hands of the reporter handling Victory Lane. More times than not, you do not get to see the real driver, their heart and soul. This is the unfortunate caveat of the (very quick) Victory Lane interview. The time restraint as well as the "lead" factor of the reporter does not allow the driver the opportunity to speak from his heart.

Girlfriend to Girlfriend

Many drivers are quite particular about the shape of the bill on the ball cap . . . You know, that ever-so-perfect curve the guys work really hard to get. If you watch the drivers in Victory Lane, you'll see many take the cap from the official, give the bill of the cap a quick squeeze, and on the head it goes.

Victory Lane Stories from NASCAR Wives

Lynn Bodine

Lynn Bodine knew her husband Todd Bodine would one day win in the Busch Series, they just didn't know when that day would come. Todd had played over in his head a million times what he would want to say if and when that time came. Enter Dover 1991. Todd took the lead from race leader Davey Allison and second place Ernie Irvan (who both ran out of gas on the final lap) to win his very first Busch race. The only problem was that Todd had become ill while driving the car and had to receive assistance to exit his car. As the live TV crews ran up to Todd for a Victory Lane interview, he slipped down beside his car with no strength to even talk. Lynn had made her way to Victory Lane by that time, so she decided to conduct the post-race Victory Lane interview herself. As her husband was propped up against the car trying to catch his breath, Lynn grabbed the microphone and proceeded to thank everyone ever associated with Todd. She even remembered to thank the sponsors. Todd never opened his mouth. To this day, Todd loves to tell everybody that he raced all those years only to have Lynn give the interview for his first win. However, he adds with a smile, "She probably did a better job than me anyway."

---

has already left the track for the airport and in some cases are on their way home via car or airplane.

The next day is full of more interviews and maybe a few words with the team. But by the time a driver reaches the next week's race venue, his win is old news.

Girlfriend to Girlfriend

Many of the drivers celebrate privately with their family sometime during the week following the race win. Some drivers have smaller more intimate get-togethers, while others "party hearty" in a big way.

New York, New York

Going to Victory Lane is fun and exciting and of course full of celebrating, but no Victory Lane celebration can match the celebrating that goes on each year in New York at the annual NASCAR Nextel Cup Awards Banquet. The awards banquet is the party of the year for the drivers, spouses, team members, sponsors, etc. The annual black-tie banquet is held each year in the historic Waldorf-Astoria in Manhattan.

The banquet is broadcast live on the first Friday night in December. The top ten drivers in points are invited (and expected), in order to receive their bonus checks on the stage and give remarks.

The Rookie of the Year and the first driver outside of the top ten (the eleventh-place finisher) are also invited to grace the stage. Many of the drivers are quite nervous with the "live" statement aspect of the show. The advice "don't let them see you sweat" would be appropriate for many of them.

Once the awards presentation is over, the ballroom is set up for the party of the year. It is customary for the newly crowned champion to host the champion's party, which means supplying the entertainment for the night. The champion's party starts immediately following the televised awards banquet. One of the most memorable champion's parties was in 2001 when then champion Jeff Gordon hired the 1970s band KC and the Sunshine Band for the entertainment. The drivers boogied to "Shake Your Booty" until the wee hours of the morning.

Girlfriend to Girlfriend

The wives love to go on the awards banquet trip because of the shopping in New York. The drivers are usually busy during the day with sponsorship commitments, so the wives get together in groups to hit the streets of New York. The bag check gets quite full.

Victory Lane Stories from NASCAR Wives

Liz Allison

It was October 7, 1990, at Lowe's Motor Speedway, one of the most popular races of the year. The Allison family owned a condo at the speedway. It was a race tradition at Charlotte to host nice parties before, during, and after the race. With that in mind, I played hostess while Davey was (obviously) racing. Because of my hostess role, I did something I would not normally do on race day: I chose to wear a dress with three-inch heels. What was I thinking? Okay, I know that does not sound smart, but I was looking good until . . . I showed my tail! Davey was the dominant car and luckily went on to win the race. Our daughter, Krista, was only a baby at the time so I was cradling her in my arms as I made my way to Victory Lane. Krista was not as excited about her daddy winning as everyone else, so I had to exit Victory Lane before Davey had even hopped out of his car. As I stepped over the beautiful shrubs surrounding Victory Lane, my three-inch heel caught the hem of my skirt. The problem was my skirt had an elastic waist. As I went to put my foot back down on the ground, my skirt decided to go south with my foot, leaving me standing in Victory Lane with a screaming baby and my skirt pulled down to my ankles . . . just me and my tail displayed to every photographer in a two-hundred-yard area. The worst part of the story is I did not have a hand available to pull my skirt back up. A very sweet security guard (in a very gentlemanly way) had to pull it back up for me. Davey loved to tell that he was surprised how excited I was . . . dropping my skirt and all.

Yes, these guys can drive, but FEW of them can dance.

While the focus of the trip is the banquet, many of the drivers and spouses make a point to catch a Broadway show and enjoy the Christmas decorations around the city. Top-name drivers are often invited to make guest stops on shows like *Live with Regis and Kelly, Good Morning America,* and *Fox and Friends.*

PART TWO

Enough Already, Let's Go Racing

CHAPTER TWELVE

Making Plans

There is no right way to experience a NASCAR race. Some people go back year after year to the same track and sit in the same seats. Others prefer to try different tracks with different types of seating. Some are happy setting up camp in the infield and never actually seeing any part of the race, while others insist on being the last person out of the stands at the conclusion of race day. The great thing about attending a NASCAR event is that there is something for everybody.

How to Purchase Tickets

NASCAR racing is becoming more and more popular every year. Because of the intense popularity and the jaw-dropping growth of the sport, the number of fans choosing to view races live has increased tremendously. The impressive TV ratings also help grow the estimated number of NASCAR fans worldwide, which is currently close to 75 million. All of this popularity, however, has made getting tickets a battle.

A large number of tracks hosting the Cup series events sell out each race, making it harder for the novice race fan to purchase tickets. The key to ticket purchasing is to *purchase early*!

Most tracks put their next season's tickets on sale the day after the most recent event. If you can plan that far ahead, make the move so you will guarantee yourself a seat in the house. Certain events, like the night race at Bristol (the Sharpie 500) and the Daytona 500, actually have a waiting list for prospective ticket buyers.

Bristol night race tickets are so hard to come by that some fans take the "worth factor" to the limit. One couple went so far as to fight over who gets the tickets in divorce proceedings. Another fan requested information from the track on how to will the tickets to his son.

Six Ways to Purchase Tickets

1. Call the track ticket office—always ask for discounts and package specials.

2. Check the track's Web site for ticket availability—some tracks set aside a certain number of seats for Web site requests.

3. Check your local newspaper's classified section for individuals selling tickets—this is most helpful with sold-out events like Bristol.

4. Check the track host city's newspaper classified for individuals wanting to sell tickets.

5. For the risk takers—attempt to purchase tickets at the race venue from fans with unused seats or from scalpers.

6. eBay is another great source for race tickets as well as hard to find tickets like Bristol, Indy, and Daytona.

Race Tip

Be careful when purchasing tickets from unknown sources like Internet sites and scalpers. Ticket counterfeiting is a problem in all sports, and NASCAR is not immune to tickets sharks.

Track Ticket Contact Numbers

Track	Ticket number	Web site
Atlanta	(770) 946-4211	www.atlantamotorspeedway.com
Bristol	(423) 764-1161	www.bristolmotorspeedway.com
California	(800) 944-7223	www.californiaspeedway.com
Chicagoland	(815) 727-7223	www.chicagolandspeedway.com
Darlington	(866) 459-7223	www.darlingtonraceway.com
Daytona	(386) 253-7223	www.daytonainternationalspeedway.com

Dover	(800) 441-7223	www.doverspeedway.com
Homestead	(305) 230-7223	www.homesteadmiamispeedway.com
Indianapolis	(317) 492-6700	www.indianapolismotorspeedway.com
Infineon	(800) 870-7223	www.infineonraceway.com
Kansas	(913) 328-7223	www.kansasspeedway.com
Las Vegas	(800) 644-4444	www.lvms.com
Lowe's (Charlotte)	(800) 455-3267	www.lowesmotorspeedway.com
Martinsville	(877) 722-3849	www.martinsvillespeedway.com
Michigan	(800) 354-1010	www.MISpeedway.com
New Hampshire	(603) 783-4931	www.nhis.com
Phoenix	(602) 252-2227	www.phoenixintlraceway.com
Pocono	(570) 646-2300	www.poconoraceway.com
Richmond	(804) 345-7223	www.rir.com
Talladega	(877) 462-3342	www.talladegasuperspeedway.com
Texas	(817) 215-8500	www.texasmotorspeedway.com
Watkins Glen	(866) 461-7223	www.theglen.com

Where to Sit

NASCAR racing is best viewed "from the top," as they say. In many other sporting arenas the better seats are close to the "ice" or "field," but not with NASCAR . . . In most cases, the higher the seat, the better. The lower seats at a track do not offer a full view of the racetrack, making it hard to see what happens on the track at all times.

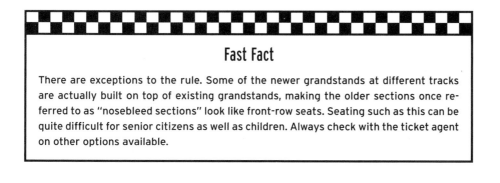

Fast Fact

There are exceptions to the rule. Some of the newer grandstands at different tracks are actually built on top of existing grandstands, making the older sections once referred to as "nosebleed sections" look like front-row seats. Seating such as this can be quite difficult for senior citizens as well as children. Always check with the ticket agent on other options available.

Many tracks have made ticket buying easy by adding a 3-D option to their Web sites. This added bonus actually allows you to see what your view is like from the seats available. The virtual ticket experience is surprisingly accurate.

Helpful Hints When Purchasing Tickets

1. Always ask for discount information.

2. Ask about weekend ticket packages—many times you can get a better rate if you buy the package deal that usually has a few bells and whistles. For instance, if you purchase a weekend pass versus a one-day ticket, the track may throw in a pit tour and special parking.

3. Ask for the last-row cutoff on a certain ticket price. You can save money by sitting one row back from the higher-dollar ticket just by sitting in the first row of the cheaper ticket area.

4. If you are planning to attend with children or if you have to use the bathroom more often, request seats at the end of the row.

5. If you are purchasing four tickets, request two seats on one row and two in the row behind, same seat numbers. This option keeps your group together, just not side by side. It is much easier to buy two and two than four in a row together.

6. If phoning in your ticket purchase, be very nice to your ticket operator—you would be surprised what they can help you with.

Special Needs

NASCAR tracks are quite handicap-capable, believe it or not. All tracks on the NASCAR circuit have reserved seating for wheelchairs and other special needs. Each track provides special handicapped parking areas to further accommodate visitors.

When traveling with someone who is handicapped or has other special needs, make sure you request track-specific information *in advance* to ensure the full advantage of all of the services available to you or someone traveling with you.

Grandstands—NASCAR, USA

The grandstands seat more fans than any other area during any given race. This is where the fan action is . . . period. Part of what makes the NASCAR race experience so much fun is meeting the people sitting around you. Most tracks seat close to 100,000 in the grandstands, while tracks like Indy seat 250,000 enthusiastic fans. Nowhere can the sights and sounds be experienced as they are in the grandstands.

Five Ways to "Fit In" with the Crowd

1. Wear your favorite driver's name or likeness on a T-shirt.

2. Stand up and cheer for your driver.

3. Be respectful of others and their choice of drivers.

4. Don't get up every two laps to go to the bathroom.

5. Dress accordingly—wear casual and comfortable clothes. Skirts, dress pants, heels, and the coat and tie need not make their way to the track.

Girlfriend to Girlfriend

I have watched races from the grandstands, pits, and suites. To me, there is no better place to be for a race than in the grandstands. My kids, Robbie and Krista, would rather be in the grandstands eating track food than in the pits any day.

Scan Me, Baby

Live NASCAR events can be extremely loud due to the roar of the cars. Take a track like Bristol—it's basically a half-mile bowl, so the roar of forty-three cars has nowhere to go. The sounds of a track bounce from one grandstand to another, one set of ears to another. During a race it is very hard to talk with the person sitting next to you, much less hear the track announcers reporting what is happening on the track. Luckily, there are a few ways to keep "up to speed" during a NASCAR race.

1. **Headset-style radios** allow you the opportunity to listen in to the national radio coverage of the race. The announcers do a great job of giving you information as it happens on the track. The announcers also give expert analysis of car problems, wrecks, etc.

2. **Racing scanners** allow you to basically "eavesdrop" in on the driver/team conversations. Scanners are available to

Girlfriend to Girlfriend

I like listening to the radio broadcast more than the scanners. However, my son, Robbie (who is fourteen), would rather listen to his favorite teams. More times than not, the younger kids do not pick up on the inappropriate language used during a race. There is usually so much going on that it goes right over their heads . . . thank goodness!

rent at all tracks, with rental prices ranging anywhere from $20 to $50. Scanners are available to purchase at the tracks as well. When renting a scanner, you will be given a driver frequency list so that you know what frequency your favorite driver is on. Even though kids love the scanners, be aware that (at times) inappropriate language is used.

The Suites—Lifestyles of the Rich and Famous

Viewing a NASCAR race from the suites is something most people will never have the opportunity to do. Suites are closed-in areas with theater seating and floor-to-ceiling glass windows, located high above the grandstands, which ultimately allows for one of the best views in the house. The suites are invitation-only, and are rented by companies and corporations who are there to wine and dine their clients and special guests. Each suite is given a certain number of suite passes that determines the total number of suite guests. The food ranges anywhere from simple finger foods to lobster and caviar.

Infield—The Lion's Den

The infield is what many consider to be the "danger zone." The "gut" of the racetrack would be more appropriate. The infield is located inside the track. Not all tracks allow general-admission infield privileges, but the ones that do are fan favorites to the "infield crowd." The infield is basically an "enter at your own risk" area set up for tents, RVs, and campers. That's where the biggest party on any given race weekend is held.

While the infield may have the best party in town, it certainly does not provide the best seat in the house. Many fans who stay in the infield see very little of the race. It is not uncommon to have an "infielder" pull out of the track on Monday morning after a race and not have any idea who finished in the top five. Some don't even know who won the race, and a few are not even sure a race took place. You get the picture!

The tracks have only a certain number of infield tickets. Always check with your track of choice way in advance for details and availability. Though the infield is quite wild, it is also quite popular. Driving miles in a camper only to find out the infield is full would throw a little water on the fire.

NASCAR's Wildest Infields

1. **Talladega.** Talladega seems to brew trouble. The county houses a temporary holding cell for fans too intoxicated to drive, or fans getting a bit too wild. How popular is the holding cell? By Monday morning there are no vacancies.

2. **Darlington.** This historic track in South Carolina is almost as famous for the stories from the infield as for the stories from the track.

3. **Daytona.** Daytona isn't referred to as "the granddaddy of tracks" for nothing. Daytona Speed Weeks lasts almost two weeks, stretching the infield party way beyond the "party limit." It takes some fans almost two more weeks to recover from the longest-running NASCAR party every year.

Girlfriend to Girlfriend

I would think long and hard before I decided to take my kids into the infield for a weekend race experience. Your kids might end up getting more of an "experience" than you bargained for. Some infields are better than others, but in general not the greatest place for kids. Always ask the track representative you receive information from on what areas (if any) are more appropriate for families with children.

Tailgating Checklist

Food

Burgers
Hamburger buns
Hot dogs
Hot-dog buns
Brats
Extra buns for brats
Baked beans
Deviled eggs
Stuffed celery with
   pimento cheese
Potato salad
Coleslaw
Chips
Salsa
Cheese dip
Cheese for burgers
Chili for hot dogs
Sauerkraut for brats
Mustard

Ketchup
Mayonnaise for deviled
   eggs
Onions
Pickles
Lettuce
Tomatoes for burgers
Relish tray
Cookies
Brownies
Rice Krispie Treats
Drinks
Ice
Rolaids

Eating Accessories

Cups
Plates
Serving plates and
   bowls

Forks
Knives
Spoons
Serving utensils
Toothpicks for relish
   tray
Napkins
Paper towels
Cooler
Garbage bags

Grilling Items

Grill
Coals
Gas tank (if needed)
Spatula
Tongs
Matches or lighter
Pans for cooking beans

Tailgating—Pass the Wings

Tailgating has become a favorite pastime of NASCAR fans. Devout tailgating fans live for the experience. Fans show up hours before a race not only to beat the race day rush, but more importantly to TAILGATE!

Tailgating takes place in the infield, camping areas, and general parking areas. What used to be the same old fare of fried chicken has now found its way to steaks on the grill. Serious tailgaters plan way in advance for where they want to park and what the menu will hold.

Some of the best food found at racetracks is served off of a tailgate. Tailgating takes place not only before a race, but often long after it was ended, as many choose to tailgate after the race while waiting for traffic to thin out.

Girlfriend to Girlfriend

Some tracks offer camping areas that are more kid-friendly. I would recommend requesting family camping information if you plan to take your children along. Camping at the track can be great fun, BUT all it takes is one wild and crazy bunch beside you to ruin your family camping experience.

Camping NASCAR-Style

All tracks on the NASCAR circuit have areas in which camping is allowed and, quite frankly, welcomed. Many retired senior citizens make their way from track to track throughout the course of the season. Some never walk through the gates of the track but are proud to make the NASCAR Cup rounds even still.

Most tracks have several camping options, from back-to-the-basics camping with a tent to special RV spots with hookups. Always contact the track you plan to visit in advance for fees, locations, and availabilities.

The Next Best Thing: How to Watch and Listen to NASCAR

Experiencing a NASCAR race in person is best, but it is not possible for most people to go to every NASCAR race.

The national coverage given to the NASCAR Nextel Cup Series is second to none. The network providers understand the importance of providing good programming to the fans, and the coverage the series receives today is the best, most complete coverage the sport has ever seen.

Watch—The Eyes See All

Fox. The Fox network, along with its cable partner FX, carries the first half of the season's races. The Fox crew is led by Mike Joy, Darrell Waltrip, and Larry McReynolds.

NBC and TNT. NBC, along with their cable partner TNT, carry the second half of the season that usually begins with the July Daytona event. The NBC/TNT broadcast places Bill Weber, Wally Dallenbach, and Benny Parsons in the booth.

The Speed Channel. The Speed Channel clearly gives race fans the most comprehensive NASCAR coverage, period, hence the name. While the Cup race is broadcast on networks, Speed covers qualifying and Happy Hour events for the Cup series. The specialty programming—which includes *Trackside, NASCAR Victory Lane, Inside Nextel Cup, NASCAR This Morning, Wind Tunnel,* and *NASCAR Nation*—gives fans an inside look into the world of NASCAR, as well as up-to-date information. The Speed Channel is the flagship station for the NASCAR Craftsman Truck Series, helping to make this specialty channel a race fan's dream. www.speedtv.com

Did you know . . .

NBC and Fox alternate the Daytona 500.

Did you know . . .

The "actor" who played Dale Earnhardt Jr. in the ESPN movie *3* is an up-and-coming driver. Chad McCumbee, twenty-one, was discovered by Barry Pepper (who portrayed Dale Earnhardt Sr.) at a driving school in North Carolina. McCumbee is racing a full-time ARCA Series car.

Fast Fact

The Speed Channel is not available in all areas. While some cable companies include Speed on regular cable, others make it an upgrade. Always check with your local cable provider for availability.

Coming in 2007

The way you see NASCAR racing will change in 2007. NBC will not return as a media partner, and ABC/ESPN will be back in the picture. This eight-year, $4.48 billion deal was announced in December 2005, validating what many already believed to be true: NASCAR racing is a hot commodity. **Fox** will be the home of the Daytona 500, the Budweiser Shootout, Daytona pole qualifying, and the first thirteen races of the NASCAR Nextel Cup Series schedule. **TNT** will air the next six consecutive NASCAR Nextel Cup Series races (races 14–19), and the remaining seventeen NASCAR Nextel Cup Series races will be broadcast on either **ABC** or **ESPN**. The final ten races (the Chase for the Championship) will be broadcast on **ABC**.

Did you know . . .

Carl Edwards was once a part-time substitute teacher in Missouri.

Listen

Motor Racing Network. MRN broadcasts the majority of the Cup Series events each year, including the Daytona 500. MRN is owned by International Speedway Corporation (see p. 8) and provides MRN affiliates with weekly favorites such as *NASCAR Live with Eli Gold* and *NASCAR Today.*

Performance Racing Network. PRN is owned by Speedway Motorsports, Inc. and is the voice for tracks like Bristol, Atlanta, Vegas, Lowe's, Texas, and Infineon. PRN is the home of *Fast Talk with Benny Parsons, PRN's Garage Pass,* and *PRN's Sunday Drive.* www.goprn.com.

Read

NASCAR Scene. A weekly-newspaper-style publication covering all of NASCAR's top three series. Very informative and great photography. 1-800-883-7323

NASCAR Illustrated. A monthly magazine covering all of NASCAR's top three. This is a high-quality glossy magazine that features behind-the-scenes stories of the drivers and excellent photography. 1-800-883-7323

Dick Berggren's Speedway Illustrated. A monthly magazine dedicated to all forms of racing. Dick Berggren is a highly respected motorsports journalist and Fox TV pit reporter. This magazine is a little more technical, with fewer photos and personal stories. 1-888-837-3684

NASCAR Preview and Press Guide. An annual magazine-style stat book with track and driver info. 1-888-747-9287

Web sites

www.NASCAR.com. The official Web site of NASCAR.

www.Jayski.com. An independent NASCAR Web site hosted by ESPN.

www.thatsracing.com. A popular unofficial NASCAR Web site.

CHAPTER THIRTEEN

Okay, Ladies, It's Time for a Road Trip!

There are many things to take into consideration when planning a NASCAR road trip, from travel arrangements and accommodations to budgets and scheduling. First, figure out which track you would like to make your race day destination. Many first-timers simply pick the track closest to them to make their live debut.

Road Trip Checklist

1. Pick race date.

2. Purchase race tickets (see "How to Purchase Tickets" in chapter 12).

3. If overnight travel is needed, make hotel reservations.

4. If air travel is necessary, book flights.

5. Book rental car (if necessary).

6. Contact local Chamber of Commerce for other activities, festivals, car shows, etc.

7. Contact track to request information on track activities, special events, autograph signings, etc.

8. Check driver Web sites for upcoming autograph sessions in that area.

9. Make dinner reservations (if needed).

10. Map out trip to and from track.

11. Check local highway department for special road closings, rerouting for race traffic, etc.

Girlfriend to Girlfriend

The airlines usually get wind of big events about two months prior to the event. Once they are aware of the race date, the fares mysteriously climb . . . and quickly. One year I booked Daytona tickets for the February event in November. A friend booked her tickets in January. Her ticket was $600 more than mine—for the same flight!

The Best-Kept Secret—*Thelma and Louise*

Who ever said a road trip had to be with your significant other? The best-kept secret is to make the road trip . . . LADIES ONLY! The age-old idea of taking a road trip with the guys is over-rated. The hardest part is convincing your husbands, boyfriends, and significant others that they'll be sitting this one out. Picture this: wide-open racing, dining, shopping, and more "people watching" than one should be allowed. What more can you ask for in a girls' trip?

Planes, Trains, and Automobiles

Not all transportation services are available at each track venue. Once you decide on your mode of transportation, call for information regarding fares, schedules, etc. Events like the Daytona 500 make for very busy flight schedules, which means sold-out flights and bumped-up rates. The best way around the fare increase and schedule dilemmas is to BOOK EARLY. The sooner the better!

Make sure you check alternative airports for better rates. Many tracks are serviced by several airports. You may have to drive a few extra miles, but it may be

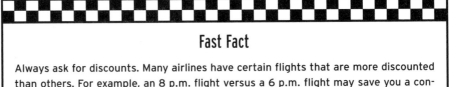

Fast Fact

Always ask for discounts. Many airlines have certain flights that are more discounted than others. For example, an 8 p.m. flight versus a 6 p.m. flight may save you a considerable amount. It's worth asking!

worth the trouble for the money you save. For example, the Daytona track is within two hours of both Orlando and Jacksonville. You are much more likely to get better rates using one of these airports instead of Daytona . . . and you stand a much better chance of getting a rental car. (For convenient airport listings see the Track Guide, appendix B.)

Airline Travel

American Airlines
    1-800-433-7300
    www.aa.com
Delta
    1-800-221-1212
    www.delta.com
Continental
    1-800-523-3273
    www.continental.com
Northwest
    1-800-225-2525
    www.nwa.com
Southwest
    1-800-435-9792
    www.southwest.com
US Airways
    1-800-438-4322
    www.usairways.com
United
    1-800-864-8331
    www.united.com

Trains

Amtrak
    1-800-872-7245
    www.amtrak.com

Rental Cars

Enterprise
    1-800-261-7331
    www.enterprise.com
Hertz
    1-800-654-3131
    www.hertz.com
Budget
    1-800-527-0700
    www.budget.com
National
    1-800-car-rent
    www.nationalcar.com
Alamo
    1-800-462-5266
    www.alamo.com

What to Wear and Pack

When going to a race, think COMFORT! You will be doing a lot of walking, so comfortable shoes are a must. Weather conditions change from track to track and region to region; whatever the case may be, dress in layers. ALWAYS, ALWAYS check the local weather report before heading out for any race. Leave a few degrees on both sides for padding. There is nothing worse than being too hot or too cold at an outdoor sporting event.

Girlfriend to Girlfriend

Always take feminine products, as most track restrooms do not have machines.

It is a good idea to take along a fanny pack or small backpack to carry all of your track essentials. Always check the track's Web site for any backpack stipulations. (See track Web sites in appendix B.)

Seat cushions are very handy and comfy for a long afternoon on the hard grandstands. Many race cushions have a handy clip to hook onto your bag or pants. Keeping your hands free is a must. You do not want to get caught carrying items around all day.

Remember . . . pack light BUT do not cut back on your race day essentials. You won't be sorry!

Track Checklist

- Race tickets
- Cash (always carry some cash for parking, etc.)
- Credit card
- Binoculars
- Seat cushion
- Sunblock
- Hat
- Earplugs
- Sunglasses
- Hand sanitizer
- Cell phone
- Race scanner—rent or buy at tracks (see chapter 12)
- Rain poncho
- Backpack
- Tampons/feminine products (there are no machines in the restrooms at most tracks)
- Extra toilet paper (just in case)
- Wet wipes—to wash hands, face, etc.

Hotel, Motel, Holiday Inn

In many cases the hardest part of your road trip is securing a hotel room. Rooms book up months in advance, with some fans returning to their hotel of choice year after year. The ever-growing number of race team members is also to blame for the shortage of hotel rooms.

Always check the area Chamber of Commerce for hotel listings. Make sure you inquire about private home, condo, and apartment rentals. This works especially well for families traveling together, or families with children.

Race Tip

Be careful when booking hotel accommodations for the dreaded "minimum night stay." Many hotels *gouge* the race fans by insisting they buy multiple nights, even if they stay for only one, as a way to meet the hotel's monthly quota (and then some!). You can get around the "minimum night stay" and expensive rooms in most cases by just staying a little farther away from the track. Usually hotels twenty or more miles from the track will not have a minimum night stay. It is worth the extra drive time to save money on hotels.

Most of the track Web sites have a hotel/accommodations link. Start at the top of the list and move down until you find a room. Be wary of some of the mom-and-pop hotels; just because the track includes the hotel on their list certainly does not mean it passed the "Mr. Clean" test. Proceed with caution! (See the Track Guide, appendix B, for hotel listings.)

Once you secure hotel accommodations you are pleased with, make sure you ask about holding your reservation for the next year. Many hotels give their current guests a courtesy "hold" for the next event. This is exactly why hotels are so hard to find. Make sure you find out the cancellation policy before you agree . . . just in case!

Dos and Don'ts of Surviving a Day at the Track

- **Do** drink LOTS of water to stay hydrated.
- **Do** remember . . . Water, beer, water, beer, water, water, beer, water (you get the idea).
- **Don't** wear makeup (okay, Tammy Faye . . . nothing worse than HOT runny makeup).
- **Do** use sunscreen (even if you think you don't need it).
- **Do** wear a hat to block the sun from beaming down on you all day.
- **Do** pack a poncho . . . just in case (a wet day at the track is not fun . . . trust me!).
- **Do** wear comfortable shoes (this is not the place to break in the cute new summer sandals).

What to Do When You Get There

In most cases there are many activities to do on race weekend besides the race itself. Many of the cities plan special events and festivals to coincide with the race.

Cities like Talladega, Charlotte, and Daytona have special museums and exhibits for the fans to experience while visiting their tracks.

It is a good idea to contact the local Chamber of Commerce (see appendix B, Track Guide, for contact information) before taking a road trip. You won't want to miss out on anything going on, from driver autograph sessions to parades.

Road Trip Grub—Eating Out

The key word here is PATIENCE! Remember, you and everybody else in town (except the locals who dare not leave their houses) are attempting to eat out. The Track Guide (appendix B) lists a few restaurants at each track. The local Chamber of Commerce is a great source for a full range of restaurants, from high-dollar to quick low-budget meals. Your hotel is another great source for restaurant info. Many tracks also have a restaurant link on their Web site with addresses and phone numbers.

Tips for Eating Out . . . NASCAR-style

- Make reservations when you can.
- Eat late—after the race day traffic has cleared.
- Break up into small groups (it is much harder to get larger tables).
- Ask about sitting at the bar (many restaurants have walk-up service available in the bar area).
- Order takeout.
- Have pizza delivered to the hotel (nothing's better than pizza and beer, poolside).
- Seek out "off the beaten path" restaurants.
- Consider hotel restaurants.
- Use room service when available.

The Top Five . . .

Driver's Wives Shopping Tracks

1. California (Fontana)
2. Infineon (Sonoma)
3. Atlanta
4. Miami
5. Richmond

Shop Till You Drop!

Shopping around NASCAR events is worth the trip. Some of the best shopping spots in the country are within a few miles of a racetrack. What better reason for a road trip than NASCAR racing and, oh yeah . . . SHOPPING!

For a list of the best shopping spots at each track, check out the Track Guide, appendix B.

CHAPTER FOURTEEN

A Day at the Races

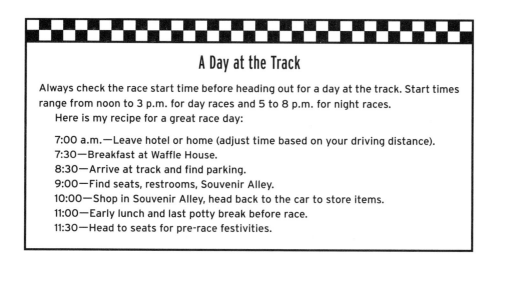

There are few things in life for a NASCAR fan that are as much fun as a day at the races. I always tell people who are new to the sport to go see a race live, though there are many different ways to see and experience a race, and many tracks to choose from. I know very few people who aren't hooked on the sport after seeing a NASCAR race up close and in person. Men ask me quite often, "How can I get my wife or girlfriend interested in racing?" My answer is always . . . take them to a race.

A Day at the Track

Always check the race start time before heading out for a day at the track. Start times range from noon to 3 p.m. for day races and 5 to 8 p.m. for night races.
Here is my recipe for a great race day:

7:00 a.m.—Leave hotel or home (adjust time based on your driving distance).
7:30—Breakfast at Waffle House.
8:30—Arrive at track and find parking.
9:00—Find seats, restrooms, Souvenir Alley.
10:00—Shop in Souvenir Alley, head back to the car to store items.
11:00—Early lunch and last potty break before race.
11:30—Head to seats for pre-race festivities.

Race Tip

If you just cannot stand to sit in traffic at the end of the day, park farther away when arriving at the track. This will make for a little longer walk, but the traffic moves more quickly farther away from the main parking areas. Another tip is to leave the race with about fifty laps to go. Most people wait until the end of the race, so leaving with fifty to go will almost guarantee a light traffic situation. If you hurry, you can catch the last few laps on the radio coverage.

T-R-A-F-F-I-C

Traffic for Nextel Cup Series races is anything but pleasurable and gives a new meaning to the phrase "Hell on Wheels!" Anytime 100,000 to 250,000 fans pile into one race venue, be ready to hurry up and wait.

The Top Five . . .

Worst Traffic Jams

1. Pocono
2. Texas
3. Atlanta
4. Dover
5. Michigan

Girlfriend to Girlfriend

Shop for NASCAR souvenirs either early in the day so you can take your purchases back to your car before the race starts, or on the way back to your car after the race is completed. Lugging around anything extra on race day is not worth the effort.

Tricks of the Trade

1. Leave early—the highest-traffic time is within four hours of the race.

2. Leave late—the lowest-traffic time is an hour before the start of the race.

3. Check highway listings for alternate routes, back roads, etc.

4. Check with your hotel for area maps and alternate routes.

5. Make sure you fill up with gas the night before.

Souvenir Alley—The NASCAR Shopping Experience

Souvenir Alley is the grandest NASCAR shopping experience you will ever encounter. Whatever a NASCAR race fan wants, Souvenir Alley delivers! Every track has an area (usually near the main grandstands) where they line up dozens of haulers (trucks) to sell driver and team goods like T-shirts, hats, etc. These haulers have a convenient pop-up side that opens up to a full view of all of the merchandise each hauler carries. The haulers accept all forms of payment, from good ol' cash to check cards and major credit cards.

Some tracks even provide cash (ATM) machines conveniently positioned near Souvenir Alley.

The Other NASCAR License

Sales for NASCAR driver's merchandise is so profitable that some individuals take it upon themselves to produce and sell merchandise bearing official logos that is not licensed by NASCAR or the drivers and car owners.

All the drivers on the NASCAR circuit license a certain company to officially produce and distribute their licensed goods. This is to protect the consumer from merchandise below the standards of what the drivers would accept for their fans.

The licensing bodies also have to pay royalties to the drivers for using their name, likeness, and signature. "Black market" providers are capitalizing on the driver's name and popularity to make a buck. This is highly frowned upon within the NASCAR ranks, so much so that if an individual or company is found to be producing or selling unauthorized and unlicensed merchandise, he or she will be arrested and stand to pay heavy fines as well as have all the goods on hand confiscated.

Fast Fact

In May 2005, law enforcement officials at Talladega Superspeedway confiscated more than 7,000 pieces of unlicensed merchandise with a value totaling close to $160,000.

In the "Pits"

Many tracks on the NASCAR circuit are now offering pre-race "pit" tours. The pre-race tour is basically a behind-the-scenes look into an area that comes to life during the race. The pit tours are usually conducted starting as early as 7 a.m. on race day, with the final tours concluding about one hour before the start of the race.

These tours are usually sold as part of weekend race packages to entice the fans to participate in all of the track's events all weekend long. Some tracks do, however, offer pit tickets separately from the package deals. Most tracks only offer a certain number of pre-race pit passes, making it imperative to inquire about pit opportunities at the earliest possible date.

Dos and Don'ts in the Pits

- **Do** stay with your tour guide if you are a part of a tour group or special group. They know how to make your trip to the "pits" enjoyable as well as informative.

- **Don't** touch any equipment in the pit stall areas. The teams are very particular about where items are placed. NASCAR officials do not have a problem with asking someone to leave who they feel has stepped out of line.

- **Do** remember the crew members are working! Race morning is very busy for the drivers and team members, only allowing them a certain amount of time to get many jobs completed. The crew members are not there to answer your race questions; they are there to do their job.

- **Do** be respectful of NASCAR officials' requests at all times. The officials are there to police not only the race but everything to do with it.

- **Do** take pictures; you might not have another chance to get that close again. Most crew members do not mind having their picture taken while working. It is, however, a nice gesture to always ask before taking a crew member's picture.

- **Do** ask for rules and regulations pertaining to children before buying pit tour tickets for them. Some tracks do not allow anyone under the age of eighteen in the pits. Always check in advance.

Garage Mania—The Driver's "Office"

The garage area is the "eye of the storm" for racing. This is a secured area where the team haulers are parked, the race cars are kept, and the teams work their magic. It is also the workplace for the drivers, an office of sorts. There is no other part of the racetrack where more official racing business takes place than in the garage area.

Because of the nature of the garage area, not everyone is allowed in. In order to enter the garage area you must have a hard card credential, a paper temporary credential, or a one-time walk-through pass. These passes are distributed by NASCAR very selectively. NASCAR will only allow sponsors and teams a certain number of passes per event to keep the total number of nonworking bystanders to a minimum. The one-time walk-through garage pass was instituted to reduce the number of fans hovering around the garage area throughout race morning.

The garage area can be a very dangerous place to be. Race cars are driving in and out of the secured area, teams are hustling tool carts, and wrenches are flying. Everyone must be careful and, most importantly, stay alert.

Dos and Don'ts in the Garage Area

Girlfriend to Girlfriend

If you ever have the opportunity to tour the garage area . . . DO IT! This is where the action is. It is most important to stay within the boundaries NASCAR has set for visitors, BUT the "wow" factor makes it worthwhile. This is as close as you can get to the action without working on the pit crew.

- **Do** be alert! Always look around you and be aware of your surroundings.
- **Don't** cross from one side of the garage area to the other without abiding by the rules of the road. Stop, look, and listen!
- **Don't** bring anyone under the age of eighteen into the garage area, unless the individual is a child of one of the drivers—NASCAR rule.
- **Don't** touch anything! The teams will not appreciate you tampering with or even touching any equipment.
- **Do** keep your garage pass visible at all times. Do not be insulted if you are questioned by a security officer or NASCAR official. Their job is to keep everyone safe and within the guidelines that NASCAR has set for the garage area.
- **Don't** approach drivers while they are with their team members. (See more about autographs later in this chapter.) Remember, this is their office and they are working.
- **Do** ask for an autograph if a driver is clearly not working and is standing near his team hauler. Most drivers have autograph cards readily available (free of charge) for the fans. The cards can be found near the back of the hauler. Quickly ask for the autograph, then move on. Do not linger to chat.
- **Don't** enter any team hauler. You will be asked to leave immediately.
- **Don't** stand close to the cars or their work areas.
- **Do** take lots of pictures.
- **Don't** consume alcohol while in the garage area, or enter while under the influence. Because of the danger factor involved in the garage area, NASCAR is very specific about what behavior will be tolerated.

Fast Fact

The "Fan Walk" at Daytona is a newer experience that epitomizes what tracks are beginning to provide for their fans. It gives fans a bird's-eye view of what is going on inside the garage area without their actually being *in* the garage area. For a minimal fee, fans can watch the teams and drivers as they work.

Girlfriend to Girlfriend

Inside scoop: the way you can tell if a driver's girlfriend is serious dating material is whether she has a hard card credential or just a temporary paper credential. A paper credential is given to people who do not have the need for a credential on a consistent basis. Get it?

Garage Area Attire

1. No shorts, capris, or skirts are allowed in the garage area. NASCAR will only permit people wearing long pants to enter.

2. No tank tops or sleeveless shirts are allowed. The rules state that all shirts must cover the shoulder.

3. No open-toed shoes such as sandals, flip-flops, etc., are allowed. All shoes must cover the toe area.

Autograph Hounds, Listen Up!

NASCAR driver autographs are highly sought after, but probably not as hard to get as you may think. It is a known fact that NASCAR drivers are more accessible than any other professional athletes. Timing and approach is everything.

Tips on Getting Autographs

1. Always keep a Sharpie pen (permanent black marker) on hand for quick autographs. If you have to search for a pen, you may lose your chance.

2. Put on your running shoes—be ready to walk along (quickly) with your driver. If he is in a hurry, you better be too.

3. Check Souvenir Alley on race morning to find out which drivers will be signing autographs on race day or even the day before the race. The drivers are set up in front of their respective trailers in order to sell goods and meet fans.

4. Contact the track before race weekend to find out about special events where drivers may be making appearances.

5. Most drivers keep an updated schedule of upcoming appearances on their Web sites.

6. The local newspapers for host cities usually have a special race section with events and other helpful information such as traffic, etc.

7. Check with the Chamber of Commerce prior to race weekend to find out about special events, including driver appearances.

8. When approaching a driver, be courteous by only asking for one autograph. There is no quicker way to get "that look" than to ask for multiple autographs.

9. Be sponsor sensitive—don't ask Dale Jr. to autograph a Coors hat.

10. If you want to have your picture taken with a driver, always ask for permission and make it quick. *Note: make sure you are not at the end of your roll of film.*

11. Always thank the driver for his or her time.

The Top Five Things Not to Say to Your Favorite Driver

1. Don't ask when he will retire.

2. Never insult his sponsor with sponsor jokes; for example . . . Viagra.

3. Don't ask him why he isn't running good.

4. Don't make comments about what you perceive as his driving ability or lack thereof.

5. Don't make negative comments about his fellow competitors.

Join the Club!

In 2004, NASCAR launched the Official NASCAR Members Club to "bring exclusive access, communication, information and racing experiences" to NASCAR fans. For an annual fee, you can be an official NASCAR member, which also comes with discounts on certain sponsor merchandise. Some lucky members can win chances to attend a drivers' meeting, be onstage during driver introductions,

Girlfriend to Girlfriend

Do not have your heart broken if your favorite driver doesn't seem so friendly when you finally get the chance to meet him or her. These drivers are incredibly busy, with lots on their minds. Remember that they are asked about five hundred times a day to sign something. It's not that they don't care or appreciate the requests, BUT after the 199th autograph it's hard to get excited.

or attend special VIP meetings with drivers. For more information visit the official site, www.NASCARmembersclub.com, or call 877-MY-NASCAR.

Driving Schools—So You Think You Want to Drive a Race Car . . .

The ol' "need for speed" leaves many fans daydreaming of climbing in the seat of a race car. Now you can experience the thrills of a race car without landing a driving contract in the Cup Series. There are several different options given to the participants at the numerous driving experiences. You can get anything from a ride in a car with an instructor to driving the car yourself. The fees range anywhere from $125 to $2,500, depending on which package you select.

Jeff Gordon Racing School	877-4-JEFF-24	www.jeffgordonracingschool.com
Dale Jarrett Racing School	888-GO-RACE-1	www.racingadventure.com
Richard Petty Driving Experience	800-BEPETTY	www.1800bepetty.com
Buck Baker Driving School	800-529-BUCK	www.buckbaker.com
Skip Barber Racing School	800-221-1131	www.skipbarber.com

CHAPTER FIFTEEN

Braving It—
Traveling with Kids

NASCAR fans under the age of sixteen are the fastest-growing demographic (along with female fans) in the sport today. The younger-generation drivers like Kasey Kahne and Dale Earnhardt Jr. have made the sport more appealing to the kid down the street.

Many believe the "redneck" image instilled in many minds in years past is now long gone, making way for a more "hip" image of the sport. Dale Earnhardt Jr. broke the mold when he announced to the world that he listens to the controversial recording artist Eminem, leaving many to wonder if the sport itself is not the only thing to leave its roots. It was just a few years back that the only music NASCAR drivers listened to was the "aw-shucks" type by artists such as Merle Haggard and George Jones. Now it's U2, 3 Doors Down, and the Black Eyed Peas.

The "hip" factor, along with the fact that NASCAR really is a family sport, is making it impossible for kids not to catch the race fever. Besides, where else can you go where virtually every member of your family can pull for someone different? Kids love the fact that they can root for their own driver regardless of who their parents like. It's their declaration of independence.

Should I or Shouldn't I?

Hmmmm, the big question . . . do I take my kids or leave them home? NASCAR racing is a family-friendly sport with a family-friendly environment (most of the time), but you should always count on a few "oops" factors along the way.

Girlfriend to Girlfriend

It is a common occurrence for children of NASCAR drivers to have a favorite driver who is not their dad. This, of course, is all in good fun, as the kids surely want their dads to win; BUT if they can't, maybe their NEXT favorite driver will win. This practice leaves many of the dads on race day wondering who their child is really pulling for.

Girlfriend to Girlfriend

I drove Robbie and Krista through the infield at Talladega one year only to be "mooned" and "flashed" before we could get from the drivers' compound to the tunnel exit. What took only minutes to drive through left me with hours of explaining to do.

Anytime beer is served in the hot sun with an average of 100,000 people, you have to be ready to do some explaining to the kids.

Many tracks now offer family grandstands, which are highly recommended for kids under fifteen. These areas are alcohol- and tobacco-free to better ensure a kid-friendly environment. Always ask for family seating when purchasing tickets for your kids. (See more on tickets in chapter 12).

The majority of race fans are very respectful of children in the grandstands, but you can never be too sure. Expect the best, but prepare for a "slip" here and there, particularly when it comes to language. Including kids on race trips is a great idea and great fun as long as you are aware of some of the issues. This is no different than any other sport, but may be revved up a few notches.

Questions to Ask When Deciding Whether to Take Your Kids

1. Can my child handle a long day at the track—walking, heat, loud noises, etc.?

2. Is there a family-friendly area for kids, for example a kids' zone?

3. Are my seats good enough for my kids to be able to see?

4. Does my child like racing enough to watch a race all day?

If you answered yes to these questions, then by all means take your kids with you.

The Top Five Most Family-Friendly Tracks

1. **Daytona.** With the addition of the Fan Walk in 2005 and the Daytona USA exhibit, as well as the beaches and the fact that Disney World is less than two hours away in nearby Orlando, Daytona leads the way for kid-friendly tracks.

2. **Lowe's Motor Speedway.** Lowe's was the front-runner in making tracks family-friendly by introducing the concept of family grandstands that are tobacco- and alcohol-free.

3. **Las Vegas.** The Vegas track is great to bring the kids to, but the city is the big kid pull. Las Vegas has more attractions and shows geared toward kids

than any other city on the Nextel Cup tour, making this a kid's top choice.

4. **Pocono.** Families (and kids) are important to the Mattioli family, who own and operate this track. The Pocono Mountains resorts are a great summer escape for the entire family.

5. **Martinsville.** This short track owns the racing world hospitality vote with its southern-style charm and family-friendly setting. Kids love this track.

What to Do When You Get There

Racetracks offer many sights and sounds that only kids can truly appreciate. A racetrack on the day of a big Nextel Cup event is more like a carnival than a track. NASCAR understands they are indeed in the entertainment business, which is reflected in all that is going on for the ticket holder on race weekends, particularly the kids.

Must-Dos at the Track

1. Check with track officials for kid activity areas. Many of these areas have kid-friendly interactive games, races, etc.

2. Always visit Souvenir Alley. (Allowance will come in handy here.)

3. Look for driver autograph postings in the souvenir area.

4. Look for simulators and other interactive games for the kids. (Many require an adult to be with the child to participate.)

5. Slot car racing is scattered throughout the fan area.

Concessions or Bust

Track concessions are like most sporting events concessions in that the food is quite expensive. Concessions are believed to produce more revenue than any other source, including ticket sales. The tracks are making big bucks because they are charging big bucks. Five dollars for a dry hamburger gives a new meaning to "highway robbery." While concessions are certainly easier than bringing your own, the price you have to pay is something to take into consideration.

Girlfriend to Girlfriend

I highly recommend leaving children under the age of four at home with a family member or babysitter. The elements of a "live" race—noise factor, long days, sun exposure, naps (more like lack thereof)—are not good for babies and small children. Trust me, you will thank me for this advice!

Girlfriend to Girlfriend

My kids love to eat race-track food, but they tend to "graze" all day, which runs up a hefty food tab. I always let my kids pick one (maybe two) things from concessions to ward off any grumblings.

Food Tips for Race Day

1. Pack sandwiches in individual bags to keep them from sticking together.

2. Stay away from items that can spoil easily, such as turkey, eggs, mayonnaise, etc.

3. Pack individual bags of chips and snacks. Look for lunchbox-size bags, available in grocery stores.

4. Pack fresh fruit—apples and oranges.

5. Stay away from chocolate chips, marshmallows, and other items that can melt.

6. Pack drink boxes and bottled water—stay away from glass items.

7. Soft drinks are not a good idea as they do not quench thirst.

8. Freeze water bottles the night before the race, pouring a little out first so the bottles don't crack. It will keep your drinks (and the food you pack with it) cold.

9. Pack protein snacks like nuts and trail mix with dried fruit and nuts.

Race Tip

Pack wet washcloths and store them in the cooler for every member of your family to cool off their faces later in the day.

What to Pack for a Day at the Races (for Your Kids)

- Tickets
- Allowance (for souvenirs)
- Binoculars
- Rain poncho
- Seat cushion
- Comfortable shoes
- Sunscreen
- Hat
- Sunglasses
- Backpack or fanny pack
- Hand sanitizer
- Earplugs
- Race scanner
- Extra toilet paper
- Baby wipes/wet washcloths
- Emergency plan and numbers to call if separated

Girlfriend to Girlfriend

You can beat the "caution flag sprint" to the bathrooms by running to the restrooms as soon as the caution flag waves. Most people wait in their seats to see what happened to bring out the caution flag. The track over-head announcer always reports what is happening on the track. You will have to hear what is going on versus seeing, BUT you will get the "happy bladder" award.

Dos and Don'ts for Kids

- **Do** make sure your child drinks lots of water—it is easier for a child to get dehydrated than an adult.
- **Do** make sure they eat throughout the day.
- **Do** reapply sunscreen several times throughout the day.
- **Do** dress them in layers as the weather can be tricky—cold in the morning, hot in the afternoon, with a rain shower in between.

Race Tip

Always, Always, Always have an emergency plan with your kids on what to do if you are separated from them. Make sure they know where to go, what to do, and who to talk to if they get away from you. It is easier than you think to get separated from someone in large crowds.

Point out track personnel and police officers as safe people to talk to. A cell phone is a good way to communicate if this happens. If you are a two-cell-phone family, give one to the kids.

Make sure the kids have a ticket stub in their pocket at all times. This will assist them in finding the seats and will help track personnel to locate you.

- **Do** rent a race scanner or take along a radio with a headset so that they can keep up with what is going on trackside.
- **Don't** allow your child to throw anything on the track—you will be escorted right out the front gates.
- **Do** insist your kids splash water on their faces on very hot days as this will help keep them cool. A cold washcloth comes in handy here as well.

Potty Time

"Potty breaks" during the day at a race can be quite the experience . . . at best! Whoever thought something so easy (and quite necessary) could be so darn COMPLICATED? Why is it that kids have to go to the bathroom three times to your one little potty break? Why is it that right when you sit back down in your seat and get comfortable, somebody needs something? And somebody please tell me why everybody has to go the bathroom at once? Ever notice how the lines are always long when you have to go to the bathroom? If only the NASCAR officials would police the bathrooms, then maybe things would move a bit quicker.

Potty Tips

1. Always pack extra toilet paper . . . just in case.

2. Hand sanitizer is a must.

3. Insist that your kids use the restroom when you do regardless of whether they feel the need.

Rescue 911

You plan all year for your great family vacation in Daytona. You have four seats at the start/finish line, the VIP pit tour, a perfect room on the beachfront in Daytona, tickets to Disney World and Sea World . . . Then, BOOM, on your first night on your perfect vacation, your child wakes up with a temperature of 104. Why is it that just when you think you have everything planned, you realize you forgot one thing—where is the closest hospital? Life will happen, as they say, and somehow with kids it seems to happen when you least expect it.

What to Do If a Crisis Happens at the Track

Every track on the NASCAR circuit has at least one first aid center. The easiest way to find it is to ask a track official or police officer. It is usually located under

Fast Fact

NASCAR drivers spend so much time at the racetrack that if they become ill they are treated by the staff in the infield care center. This is true for the drivers' families and crew members as well. This care center basically is a doctor's office/trauma unit for anyone needing medical assistance at the racetrack. NASCAR drivers have been treated there for strep throat, stomach viruses, and just about everything in between. Over my years in the sport, I have been treated for a bee sting, a deep cut on my ankle (from a pit cart), and even premature contractions.

the main grandstands. Larger tracks have several centers set up around the facility. The first aid areas are primarily for minor and non-life-threatening situations, with the most common requests being for Tylenol, aspirin, Band-Aids, etc. More serious conditions are handled by the emergency workers on site. Ambulances are always readily available to transport patients to nearby hospitals if necessary.

All tracks on the NASCAR circuit have "infield care centers," which are state-of-the-art trauma units, including air transport capabilities, intended mainly to treat driver injuries. But they certainly treat ticket buyers if the need should arise. These trauma units are located in the infield of each track facility. They are equipped by local hospitals, with a full staff of nurses, doctors, and specialists. If someone should experience a more serious situation at a track, they will be advised to visit the infield care center or be transported to a nearby hospital for further evaluation or treatment.

What to Do If a Crisis Happens at the Hotel

Murphy's Law loves vacations! What "could," but "shouldn't," but "maybe will," just *somehow happens*. Confucius says, "Plan for it and it won't happen." If in fact ol' Murphy comes calling while you are visiting a race town, not to fret. The NASCAR tour is not at a loss for hospitals.

If an emergency situation arises, check with your hotel manager on your quickest route to the hospital. If the situation needs immediate care . . . *call for ambulance service.* Don't try to drive in unknown territory.

For the addresses and phone numbers of track-area hospitals, please see the Track Guide, appendix B.

Girlfriend to Girlfriend

Robbie and Krista certainly made their faces known to several of the emergency rooms around the NASCAR tour. Rockingham, Bristol, Florence, and Richmond are all emergency rooms we visited for various reasons. Robbie conveniently stuffed a (very large) glob of Play-Doh in his nose in Darlington one year. Davey returned to the hotel after a long day at the track, only to track us down in the emergency room. Of course, he proceeded to sign autographs for the nursing staff while also tending to our son.

CHAPTER SIXTEEN

Come on, Girls, Let's Have a Party

Now that you have learned the ropes of racing, it is time to "strut your stuff." What better way to show off your new NASCAR knowledge than to throw a NASCAR viewing party.

How to Plan a NASCAR Party

Planning a NASCAR-themed party is almost as fun as hosting it. When making your invitations list, make sure you invite people who are fun; no knuckleheads, please! You should plan for the party to begin about thirty minutes before the pre-race TV coverage starts. Customarily the pre-race begins about an hour before the green flag waves, but check your local listings as the times vary from week to week.

Party Checklist
- Make your guest list.
- Pick a date (check time and TV listing for race broadcast).
- Order invitations or print your own.
- Mail invitations two weeks prior to your party.
- Make menu choices.
- Plan your party (but go with the flow).
- Shop for door prizes, paper products, and decorating items.
- Shop for food and drinks.

- Prepare food.
- Decorate home.
- Party hearty!

The Invite

Ladies, it's time to throw the green flag on your party. The first thing you need to decide is whether you want to send out invitations. If it is a last-minute, low-key thing, don't bother. But if you want to go all out . . . do the invites.

Many print shops have great-looking race-themed papers to print on. Remember that the key colors here are red, black, and white. You can always throw in green and yellow for more color. For you computer-savvy ladies, the sky's the limit . . . think racey!

Race Tip

Any color used on the NASCAR flags is acceptable for invitations: black, white, red, yellow, or green.

The Top Five Invite Choices

1. Red invites with checkered borders.
2. White invites with checkered borders.
3. Solid black paper with silver Sharpie to print party details.
4. White invites with NASCAR flags for borders.
5. Solid white notecard-style invites with black borders and red text.

Decorating Tips

The key to decorating for a race-themed party is staying with the racing colors—red, black, and white with a shot of green and yellow. A very easy way to decorate with race colors is with the paper products and utensils you use.

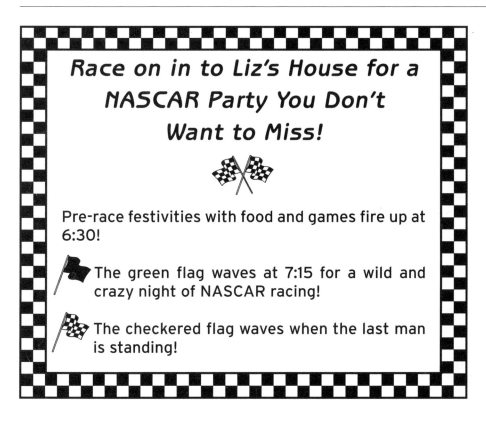

Napkins. Red and black napkins are the best choice if you cannot find any checkered-flag napkins. Mix the red and black napkins to give them a little pizzazz.

Plates. Paper plates are a must because of the ease of throwing them away. You cannot go wrong with red and black plates. Again, mixing the colors is a good choice.

Utensils. You can use your own or purchase red and black plastic. Clear or white plastic will work as well.

Cups. You can use your own, but why not make it easy and go for the throwaway? Stay with the black-and-red theme or clear plastic. A fun way to personalize your guests' drinking cups is to cut out drivers' pictures from race magazines and tape the pictures to the cups with your guests' names. They have to be that driver for the day.

Flags. Many party stores have checkered flags for sale. They are inexpensive paper flags that look great and add a lot of color to your party; use them as props around the house. They are easy to stick in flower arrangements, put over the mantel, or drop in a vase. Always attach a flag to the mailbox so that your guests get the racing feel before they even walk in the door.

Girlfriend to Girlfriend

Checkered Flags are a "must" for NASCAR parties. Remember, presentation is everything!

Balloons. Balloons are a must for a party geared toward kids. There is nothing catchier than red, black, white, green, and yellow balloons. Balloons work for adult parties as well, and are great for the mailbox.

Cars. Matchbox race cars and die-cast cars make great centerpieces and companion decorating items. The best place to purchase these cars is at discount stores and race shops. The cars come in a variety of sizes and colors. You can use construction paper to write the names of your guests and tape to Matchbox cars for eye-catching nameplates.

NASCAR "Racey" Recipes

Let's get one thing straight—everyone is there to watch the race, but food is always a must. Depending on the time of the race, it may or may not be suitable for a full-course meal. Finger foods are a great choice for any party, especially NASCAR-themed finger foods. There won't be any cautions thrown on this menu.

Pit Road Cheese Ball

2 8-ounce packages of cream cheese
8 ounces New York sharp cheddar, grated
1 large onion, grated
salt to taste
dash cayenne pepper
½ cup chopped parsley
½ cup chopped pecans
paprika

Mix the cheeses and onion by hand. Add salt and pepper. Mix again and place in a bowl, then cover with plastic wrap. Refrigerate for 3 hours. Form the cheese into a ball and roll the ball in the parsley and nuts. Sprinkle with paprika. Serve with your favorite crackers.

Caution Bourbon Hot Dogs

1 pound hot dogs, cut in chunks
1½ cups ketchup
¾ cup bourbon
½ cup dark brown sugar

Mix all the ingredients and simmer over low heat in a heavy skillet or
Crock-Pot for 6 to 8 hours.

Red Flag Barbecue Meatballs

1½ pounds ground round
½ cup uncooked oatmeal
½ cup milk
1 egg, beaten
¼ cup minced onion
2 tablespoons parsley, chopped
1 teaspoon salt
⅛ teaspoon pepper

Combine all the ingredients until thoroughly blended. Shape into 1-inch
meatballs. Brown on all sides in a large skillet over medium heat. Drain
the fat.

Sauce

1 10-ounce jar grape jelly
1 bottle chili sauce

Combine the ingredients and pour over the meatballs. Bring to a boil.
Reduce heat and simmer for 20 minutes.

Green Flag Artichoke Dip

1 can artichoke hearts, chopped and drained
1 cup mayonnaise
1 cup parmesan cheese
pinch cayenne pepper

Mix all the ingredients. Pour into a round casserole dish. Cook at 350°F
until bubbly. Serve with tortilla chips. (Mix blue corn and white corn
tortilla chips if you want to make it more fun.)

Green-and-White-Checkered Cucumber Dip

½ cucumber, unpeeled
1 8-ounce package cream cheese
¼ teaspoon dill
dash garlic salt
2 tablespoons mayonnaise

Finely grate the cucumber. Blend all the ingredients until creamy. Serve with your favorite crackers or use as a nice spread for mini sandwiches.

White Flag Cottage Cheese Salad

1 pound cottage cheese
1 small bag miniature white marshmallows
1 small can crushed pineapple, drained
1 jar cherries
1 carton Cool Whip

Mix all the ingredients and chill for 1 hour.

Victory Lane Chip Bars

2⅓ cups sifted all-purpose flour
½ teaspoon baking powder
¼ teaspoon salt
1 cup butter or margarine
1 cup brown sugar
1 teaspoon vanilla extract
¾ cup chopped pecans
1 12-ounce package chocolate chips

Preheat the oven to 350°F. Sift the flour, baking powder, and salt. In a separate bowl, beat together the butter, sugar, and vanilla. Add the dry ingredients and mix well. Stir in the nuts and chocolate chips. Press the dough firmly into a well-greased baking pan. Bake for 20 minutes or until lightly browned. While still hot, cut into bars.

Restrictor-Plate Cookies

12 ounces chocolate chips
12 ounces butterscotch morsels
6 ounces chow mein noodles
1½ cups dry-roasted peanuts

In a heavy saucepan melt the chocolate chips and butterscotch morsels. Add the noodles and nuts until well blended. Drop on wax paper and refrigerate for 30 minutes.

Racey Punch

6 cups cranberry juice
3 cups apple juice
¾ cup lemon juice
1½ cups orange juice
1 quart ginger ale

Mix together and chill. This is a great punch to "spike" if you feel the need.

Party Tip

Make sure you load up on the drinks; always have beer and sodas on hand.

Oh, the Games People Play

Ask your guests to arrive about thirty minutes to an hour before the race starts. This gives everyone a chance to eat, mingle, and settle in for the race. Once all your guests have arrived . . . let the games begin!

Have everyone write their names and their predictions of which driver will win on a piece of paper. Everyone should put their paper in a bowl, to be looked at only after the race. Ask everyone to throw in $5 . . . this revs up the competition factor. If there is a tie, the money pot is split between however many people picked the winner.

While the winning driver is the only money-pot game, you can keep things hopping by having other fun games going on throughout the race. The secondary games are where you can have some fun with door prizes. Some options for guessing games are:

You might be a female NASCAR fan if . . .

You issue a red flag to your husband for planning a race trip without you.

- Who will be the first driver to fall out of the race?
- Who will be the best-finishing rookie?
- How many laps until the first caution?
- Who will lead the most laps?
- Who will lead the race at the halfway mark?
- How many cautions will be in the race?
- Who will cause "the Big One"?

If you want an alternative to making predictions, how about a wild and crazy game of "pin the driver on the car" (blindfold and all)?

The Prize Stash

Door prizes should be inexpensive and fun. The best place to shop for NASCAR-themed door prizes is at a racing/souvenir store. Check your yellow pages for store listings and locations. If time allows, you can find whatever your heart desires online. You should expect to wait at least two weeks for delivery of ordered items.

"Racey" Door Prizes
- Earplugs
- Race-themed beer koozies
- NASCAR keychains
- NASCAR car flags
- NASCAR bumper stickers
- A NASCAR pacifier or bib for the party's biggest "baby"
- NASCAR bandannas
- NASCAR lapel pins
- NASCAR writing pens
- NASCAR toy cars

The NASCAR Trivia Challenge

Make photocopies of the quiz sheet on the next page to hand out to your guests to test their NASCAR knowledge. Answers are in the back of the book in appendix E.

The NASCAR Trivia Challenge

1. What driver has the most Daytona 500 wins?

2. What track hosted the race dubbed "One Hot Night" in 1992?

3. What former Cup Series driver nicknamed Cup Series regular Joe Nemechek "Front Row Joe"?

4. What veteran driver was nicknamed "Mr. September"?

5. How many Daytona 500 starts did it take Darrell Waltrip to finally win the coveted trophy?

6. What current Cup-level car owner participates in amateur boxing in his off time?

7. What driver is known as "Rocket Man"?

8. What current driver endorses Halston Z-14 cologne?

9. Who are the founders of the Victory Junction Gang Camp?

10. What track hosts the Gatorade Duals?

11. What is the nickname of car owner Jack Roush?

12. What Cup Series competitor is also known as "Smoke"?

PART THREE

The Nuts and Bolts

The Movers and Shakers

One of the most exciting things about NASCAR is the interesting personalities behind the wheels of the cars. There is certainly somebody for everyone. NASCAR drivers come and go, but the one thing that stays consistent is the drivers' intense desire to succeed at stock car racing's top level. Thousands of race car drivers dream of making it to the big time; few of them ever see their dreams come true.

Current Nextel Cup Drivers

John Andretti

Date of birth: March 12, 1963
Hometown: Indianapolis, Indiana
Resides: Mooresville, North Carolina
Marital status: Married, wife Nancy
Children: Jarrett, Olivia, Amelia
Height: 5'5"
Weight: 140 pounds
Hobbies: Playing the stock market
Web site: http://www.nascar.com/drivers/dps/jandrett00/cup/index.html
Fan club: John Andretti Fan Club
          PO Box 2104
          Davidson, NC 28036

Greg Biffle

Date of birth: December 23, 1969
Hometown: Vancouver, Washington
Resides: Mooresville, North Carolina
Marital status: Single
Children: None
Height: 5'9"
Weight: 170 pounds
Hobbies: Flying, boating
Web site: http://www.roushracing.com/greg_biffle/
Fan club: www.gregbiffle.com

Dave Blaney

Date of birth: October 24, 1962
Hometown: Hartford, Ohio
Resides: Trinity, North Carolina
Marital status: Married, wife Lisa
Children: Emma, Ryan, Erin
Height: 5'8"
Weight: 170 pounds
Hobbies: Basketball, working with his World of Outlaws sprint car team
Web site: www.daveblaney.com
Fan club: PO Box 470142
            Tulsa, OK 74147

Mike Bliss

Date of birth: April 5, 1965
Hometown: Milwaukie, Oregon
Resides: Milwaukie, Oregon
Marital Status: Married, wife Sue
Children: Brittney
Height: 6'1"
Weight: 190 pounds
Hobbies: Boating, fishing
Web site: www.mikebliss.com
Fan club: www.mikebliss.com

Clint Bowyer

Date of birth: May 30, 1979
Hometown: Emporia, Kansas
Resides: Welcome, North Carolina
Marital status: Single
Children: None
Height: 5'11"
Weight: 180 pounds
Hobbies: Old cars, lake life
Web site: www.clintbowyer.com
Fan club: www.clintbowyer.com

Jeff Burton

Date of birth: June 26, 1967
Hometown: South Boston, Virginia
Resides: Cornelius, North Carolina
Marital status: Married, wife Kim
Children: Kimberle, Harrison
Height: 5'7"
Weight: 155 pounds
Hobbies: Golf, boating
Web site: www.jeffburton.com
Fan club: Jeff Burton Fan Club
                PO Box 339
                Harrisburg, NC 28075

Ward Burton

Date of birth: October 25, 1961
Hometown: South Boston, Virginia
Resides: Halifax, Virginia
Marital status: Married, wife Tabitha
Children: Sarah, Jeb, Everett
Height: 5'6"
Weight: 150 pounds
Hobbies: Hunting and outdoor activities
Web site: www.wardburton.com

Fan club: Ward Burton Fan Club
PO Box 295
Halifax, VA 24558

Kurt Busch

Date of birth: August 4, 1978
Hometown: Las Vegas, Nevada
Resides: Concord, North Carolina
Marital status: Single
Children: None
Height: 5'11"
Weight: 150 pounds
Hobbies: Jet skiing, water skiing, snow skiing
Web site: www.kurtbusch.com
Fan club: www.kurtbusch.com

Kyle Busch

Date of birth: May 2, 1985
Hometown: Las Vegas, Nevada
Resides: Las Vegas, Nevada
Marital status: Single
Children: None
Height: 6'1"
Weight: 160 pounds
Hobbies: Playing Xbox, *NASCAR Thunder*
Web site: http://www.nascar.com/drivers/dps/kbusch01/cup/index.html
Fan club: Kyle Busch Fan Club
PO Box 1225
Harrisburg, NC 28075

Dale Earnhardt Jr.

Date of birth: October 10, 1974
Hometown: Kannapolis, North Carolina
Resides: Mooresville, North Carolina
Marital status: Single
Children: None
Height: 6'0"
Weight: 165 pounds

Hobbies: Car restoration, music, computers, video games

Web site: www.dalejr.com

Fan club: Club E Jr.

       PO Box 5190

       Concord, NC 28027

Carl Edwards

Date of birth: August 15, 1979

Hometown: Columbia, Missouri

Resides: Mooresville, North Carolina

Marital status: Single

Children: None

Height: 6'1"

Weight: 185 pounds

Hobbies: Racing

Web site: http://www.roushracing.com/carl_edwards/

Fan club: http://www.roushracing.com/carl_edwards/

Bill Elliott

Date of birth: October 8, 1955

Hometown: Dawsonville, Georgia

Resides: Blairsville, Georgia

Marital status: Married, wife Cindy

Children: Starr, Brittany, Chase

Height: 6'1"

Weight: 185 pounds

Hobbies: Skiing, snowboarding, flying

Web site: www.billelliott.com

Fan club: The Bill Elliott Fan Club

       c/o Ignition, Inc.

       512 Means Street, Suite 200

       Atlanta, GA 30318

Jeff Gordon

Date of birth: August 4, 1971

Hometown: Vallejo, California

Resides: Charlotte, North Carolina

Marital status: Single

Children: None
Height: 5'7"
Weight: 150 pounds
Hobbies: Skiing, video games, golf, racquetball, bowling, scuba diving
Web site: www.jeffgordon.com
Fan club: Jeff Gordon Fan Club
          PO Box 910
          Harrisburg, NC 28075

Robby Gordon

Date of birth: January 2, 1969
Hometown: Cerritos, California
Resides: Orange, California, and Parker, Arizona
Marital status: Single
Children: None
Height: 5'10"
Weight: 180 pounds
Hobbies: Boating, mountain biking, waterskiing
Web site: www.robbygordon.com
Fan club: www.robbygordon.com

Jeff Green

Date of birth: September 6, 1962
Hometown: Owensboro, Kentucky
Resides: Davidson, North Carolina
Marital status: Married, wife Michelle
Children: None
Height: 5'8"
Weight: 190 pounds
Hobbies: Hunting, radio-controlled cars
Web site: www.jeffgreen.com
Fan club: Jeff Green Fan Club
          PO Box 268
          Cornelius, NC 28031

Bobby Hamilton Jr.

Date of birth: January 8, 1978
Hometown: Nashville, Tennessee

Resides: Nashville, Tennessee
Marital status: Married, wife Stephanie
Children: Haley
Height: 5'5"
Weight: 170 pounds
Hobbies: Racing, paintball guns
Web site: www.bobbyhamiltonjr.com
Fan club: www.bobbyhamiltonjr.com/fan_club.htm

Denny Hamlin

Date of birth: November 18, 1980
Hometown: Chesterfield, Virginia
Resides: Davidson, North Carolina
Marital status: Single
Children: None
Height: 6'0"
Weight: 170 pounds
Hobbies: Online racing
Web site: www.dennyhamlin.com
Fan club:www.dennyhamlin.com

Kevin Harvick

Date of birth: December 8, 1975
Hometown: Bakersfield, California
Resides: Winston-Salem, North Carolina
Marital status: Married, wife DeLana
Children: None
Height: 5'10"
Weight: 175 pounds
Hobbies: Radio-controlled race cars
Web site: www.kevinharvick.com
Fan club: Kevin Harvick Fan Club
        703 Park Lawn Court
        Kernersville, NC 27284

Dale Jarrett

Date of birth: November 26, 1956
Hometown: Hickory, North Carolina

Resides: Hickory, North Carolina
Marital status: Married, wife Kelley
Children: Jason, Natalee, Karsyn, Zachary
Height: 6'2"
Weight: 215 pounds
Hobbies: Golf
Web site: www.dalejarrett.com
Fan club: Dale Jarrett Fan Club
       1915 Fairgrove Church Road SE
       Newton, NC 28658

Jimmie Johnson

Date of birth: September 17, 1975
Hometown: El Cajon, California
Resides: Mooresville, North Carolina
Marital status: Married, wife Chandra
Children: None
Height: 5'11"
Weight: 175 pounds
Hobbies: Water sports
Web site: www.lowesracing.com
Fan club: www.jimmiejohnson.com

Kasey Kahne

Date of birth: April 10, 1980
Hometown: Enumclaw, Washington
Resides: Huntersville, North Carolina
Marital status: Single
Children: None
Height: 5'8"
Weight: 150 pounds
Hobbies: Snowmobiles
Web site: www.kaseykahne.com
Fan club: Kasey Kahne Fan Club
       10 W. Market St.,
       Suite 1026
       Indianapolis, IN 46205

Matt Kenseth

Date of birth: March 10, 1972
Hometown: Cambridge, Wisconsin
Resides: Terrell, North Carolina
Marital status: Married, wife Katie
Children: Ross
Height: 5'9"
Weight: 150 pounds
Hobbies: Motorcycling, boating, golf, computer games
Web site: www.mattkenseth.com
Fan club: Matt Kenseth Fan Club
         10 Water Street
         Cambridge, WI 53523

Travis Kvapil

Date of birth: March 1, 1976
Hometown: Janesville, Wisconsin
Resides: Janesville, Wisconsin
Marital status: Married, wife Jennifer
Children: Kelsey, Carson
Height: 6'0"
Weight: 190 pounds
Hobbies: Watching the Green Bay Packers
Web site: www.traviskvapil.com
Fan club: www.traviskvapil.com

Bobby Labonte

Date of birth: May 8, 1964
Hometown: Corpus Christi, Texas
Resides: Trinity, North Carolina
Marital status: Married, wife Donna
Children: Robert, Madison
Height: 5'9"
Weight: 175 pounds
Hobbies: Fishing
Web site: www.bobbylabonte.com

Fan club: Bobby Labonte Fan Club
PO Box 358
Trinity, NC 27370

Terry Labonte

Date of birth: November 16, 1956
Hometown: Corpus Christi, Texas
Resides: Thomasville, North Carolina
Marital status: Married, wife Kim
Children: Justin, Kristen
Height: 5'10"
Weight: 165 pounds
Hobbies: Hunting, fishing
Web site: www.terrylabonte.com
Fan club: Terry Labonte Fan Club
PO Box 579
Harrisburg, NC 28075

Jason Leffler

Date of birth: September 16, 1975
Hometown: Indianapolis, Indiana
Resides: Long Beach, California
Marital status: Married, wife Alison
Children: None
Height: 5'3"
Weight: 130 pounds
Hobbies: Boating, video games
Web site: www.jasonleffler.com
Fan club: www.jasonleffler.com

Sterling Marlin

Date of birth: June 30, 1957
Hometown: Columbia, Tennessee
Resides: Columbia, Tennessee
Marital status: Married, wife Paula
Children: Steadman, Sutherlin
Height: 6'0"

Weight: 180 pounds

Hobbies: Civil War history, collecting artifacts, following University of Tennessee football

Web site: http://www.nascar.com/drivers/dps/smarlin00/cup/index.html

Fan club: The Sterling Marlin Fan Club
      PO Box 1100
      Pulaski, TN 38478

Mark Martin

Date of birth: January 9, 1959

Hometown: Batesville, Arkansas

Resides: Daytona Beach, Florida

Marital status: Married, wife Arlene

Children: Amy, Rachel, Heather, Stacy, Matt

Height: 5'6"

Weight: 135 pounds

Hobbies: Weight training, quarter-midget racing with his son

Web site: www.markmartin.com

Fan club: www.markmartin.com

Jeremy Mayfield

Date of birth: May 27, 1969

Hometown: Owensboro, Kentucky

Resides: Mooresville, North Carolina

Marital status: Married, wife Shana

Children: None

Height: 6'0"

Weight: 190 pounds

Hobbies: Four-wheel vehicles

Web site: www.jeremymayfield.com

Fan club: Jeremy Mayfield Fan Club
      PO Box 2365
      Cornelius, NC 28031

Jamie McMurray

Date of birth: June 3, 1976

Hometown: Joplin, Missouri

Resides: Concord, North Carolina
Marital status: Single
Children: None
Height: 5'8"
Weight: 150 pounds
Hobbies: Radio-controlled cars
Web site: www.jamiemcmurray.com
Fan club: Jamie McMurray Fan Club
      PO Box 5034
      Concord, NC 28027

Casey Mears

Date of birth: March 12, 1978
Hometown: Bakersfield, California
Resides: Huntersville, North Carolina
Marital status: Single
Children: None
Height: 5'8"
Weight: 158 pounds
Hobbies: Wakeboarding, snowboarding
Web site: www.caseymears.com
Fan club: www.caseymears.com

Joe Nemechek

Date of birth: September 26, 1963
Hometown: Lakeland, Florida
Resides: Mooresville, North Carolina
Marital status: Married, wife Andrea
Children: John, Blair, Kennedy
Height: 5'9"
Weight: 185 pounds
Hobbies: Fishing, skiing
Web site: www.joenemechek.com
Fan club: JNFC
      PO Box 1131
      Mooresville, NC 28115

Ryan Newman

Date of birth: December 8, 1977
Hometown: South Bend, Indiana
Resides: Sherrills Ford, North Carolina
Marital status: Married, wife Krissie
Children: None
Height: 5'11"
Weight: 207 pounds
Hobbies: Fishing, radio-controlled cars
Web site: http://www.nascar.com/drivers/dps/rnewman00/cup/index.html
Fan club: Ryan Newman Fan Club
　　　　　PO Box 3718
　　　　　South Bend, IN 46619

Kyle Petty

Date of birth: June 20, 1960
Hometown: Trinity, North Carolina
Resides: Trinity, North Carolina
Marital status: Married, wife Pattie
Children: Adam, Austin, Montgomery
Height: 6'2"
Weight: 195 pounds
Hobbies: Reading, riding motorcycles, collecting books, collecting Elvis
　　memorabilia
Web site: www.pettyracing.com
Fan club: Kyle Petty Fan Club
　　　　　135 Longfield Dr.
　　　　　Mooresville, NC 28115

Scott Riggs

Date of birth: January 1, 1971
Hometown: Bahama, North Carolina
Resides: Bahama, North Carolina
Marital status: Married, wife Jai
Children: Layne
Height: 5'6"
Weight: 175 pounds
Hobbies: Horseback riding, riding dirt and road bikes, water sports

Web site: http://www.nascar.com/drivers/dps/sriggs00/cup/index.html
Fan club: MBV/MB2 Motorsports
      Attn: Scott Riggs
      7065 Zephyr Place NW
      Concord, NC 28027

Elliott Sadler

Date of birth: April 30, 1975
Hometown: Emporia, Virginia
Resides: Emporia, Virginia
Marital status: Single
Children: None
Height: 6'2"
Weight: 195 pounds
Hobbies: Golf, hunting, basketball, water sports
Web site: http://www.nascar.com/drivers/dps/esadler00/cup/index.html
Fan club: Elliott Sadler Fan Club
      PO Box 32
      Emporia, VA 23847

Ken Schrader

Date of birth: May 29, 1955
Hometown: Fenton, Missouri
Resides: Concord, North Carolina
Marital status: Married, wife Ann
Children: Dorothy Lynn, Sheldon
Height: 5'9"
Weight: 200 pounds
Hobbies: Driving in a number of race series, riding dirt bikes and motorcycles
Web site: www.schraderracing.com
Fan club: Ken Schrader Fan Club
      PO Box 5430
      Concord, NC 28027

Brent Sherman

Date of birth: May 24, 1974
Hometown: St. Paul, Minnesota
Resides: Concord, North Carolina

Marital status: Single
Children: None
Height: 5'6"
Weight: 180 pounds
Hobbies: Computer games
Web site: www.brentsherman.com
Fan club: www.brentsherman.com

Reed Sorenson

Date of birth: February 5, 1986
Hometown: Peachtree City, Georgia
Resides: Concord, North Carolina
Marital status: Single
Children: None
Height: 5'10"
Weight: 165 pounds
Hobbies: Weight lifting, video games, water sports
Web site: www.reedsorenson.com
Fan club: www.reedsorenson.com

Tony Stewart

Date of birth: May 20, 1971
Hometown: Rushville, Indiana
Resides: Columbus, Indiana, and Cornelius, North Carolina
Marital status: Single
Children: None
Height: 5'9"
Weight: 170 pounds
Hobbies: Pool, bowling, boating, fishing
Web site: www.tonystewart.com
Fan club: Tony Stewart Fan Club
            5671 W. 74th St. (Park 100)
            Indianapolis, IN 46278

David Stremme

Date of birth: June 19, 1977
Hometown: South Bend, Indiana
Resides: Mooresville, North Carolina

Marital status: Single
Children: None
Height: 5'11"
Weight: 175 pounds
Hobbies: Snowmobiles, mountain biking, inline-skating
Web site: www.davidstremme.net
Fan club: www.davidtsremme.net

Martin Truex Jr.

Date of birth: June 29, 1980
Hometown: Mayetta, New Jersey
Resides: Mooresville, North Carolina
Marital status: Single
Children: none
Height: 5'11"
Weight: 180 pounds
Hobbies: Fishing, hunting, four-wheeling, snowmobiles, computer racing games
Web site: www.martintruexjr.com
Fan club: www.martintruexjr.com

Brian Vickers

Date of birth: October 24, 1983
Hometown: Thomasville, North Carolina
Resides: Thomasville, North Carolina
Marital status: Single
Children: None
Height: 5'11"
Weight: 160 pounds
Hobbies: Golf, video games
Web site: www.brianvickers.com
Fan club: Brian Vickers Fan Club
　　　　27 High Tech Blvd.
　　　　Thomasville, NC 27360

Mike Wallace

Date of birth: March 10, 1969
Hometown: St. Louis, Missouri
Resides: St. Louis, Missouri

Marital status: Married, wife Carla
Children: Lyndsey, Christina, Matthew, Ryan
Height: 6'0"
Weight: 220 pounds
Hobbies: Flying, working with heavy equipment
Web site: www.mikewallace.com
Fan club: Mike Wallace Fan Club
      PO Box 4450
      Mooresville, NC 28117

Michael Waltrip

Date of birth: April 30, 1963
Hometown: Owensboro, Kentucky
Resides: Sherrills Ford, North Carolina
Marital status: Married, wife Elizabeth "Buffy"
Children: Caitlin, Margaret
Height: 6'5"
Weight: 210 pounds
Hobbies: Running, golf, tennis, boating
Web site: www.michaelwaltrip.com
Fan club: Michael Waltrip Fan Club
      PO Box 5065
      Concord, NC 28027

Scott Wimmer

Date of birth: January 26, 1976
Hometown: Wausau, Wisconsin
Resides: High Point, North Carolina
Marital status: Single
Children: None
Height: 6'0"
Weight: 180 pounds
Hobbies: Hunting and fishing
Web site: www.scottwimmer.com
Fan club: www.scottwimmer.com

Modern-Era Champions, 1972–2005

1972—Richard Petty	1989—Rusty Wallace
1973—Benny Parsons	1990—Dale Earnhardt
1974—Richard Petty	1991—Dale Earnhardt
1975—Richard Petty	1992—Alan Kulwicki
1976—Cale Yarborough	1993—Dale Earnhardt
1977—Cale Yarborough	1994—Dale Earnhardt
1978—Cale Yarborough	1995—Jeff Gordon
1979—Richard Petty	1996—Terry Labonte
1980—Dale Earnhardt	1997—Jeff Gordon
1981—Darrell Waltrip	1998—Jeff Gordon
1982—Darrell Waltrip	1999—Dale Jarrett
1983—Bobby Allison	2000—Bobby Labonte
1984—Terry Labonte	2001—Jeff Gordon
1985—Darrell Waltrip	2002—Tony Stewart
1986—Dale Earnhardt	2003—Matt Kenseth
1987—Dale Earnhardt	2004—Kurt Busch
1988—Bill Elliott	2005—Tony Stewart

All-Time Wins

Driver	Wins
Richard Petty	200
David Pearson	105
Bobby Allison	84
Darrell Waltrip	84
Cale Yarborough	83
Dale Earnhardt	76
Jeff Gordon	73
Lee Petty	55
Rusty Wallace	55
Ned Jarrett	50
Junior Johnson	50

Money, Honey: The All-Time Money Leaders

Driver	Amount
Jeff Gordon	$66,964,439
Dale Jarrett	$46,915,666
Mark Martin	$46,135,779
Rusty Wallace	$43,670,500
Dale Earnhardt Sr.	$41,742,384
Bobby Labonte	$40,843,154
Terry Labonte	$37,809,799
Bill Elliott	$36,995,303
Ricky Rudd	$36,120,592
Jeff Burton	$35,642,417
Tony Stewart	$34,905,161
Sterling Marlin	$32,970,362
Dale Earnhardt Jr.	$29,555,869
Michael Waltrip	$27,640,029
Matt Kenseth	$26,501,894

Where the Rubber Meets the Road

As every track is unique, so are the towns that host each event. This is your handy guide to each track. It will tell you everything from where to stay to how to get race tickets and what to do when you get there. Always check with the local-area Chamber of Commerce for full hotel and restaurant listings as well as events, autograph sessions, and festivals. Each track section will include:

- Track information
- Ticket information number
- Hotel listings
- Local Chamber of Commerce
- Closest hospitals
- Area restaurants
- Airports serving the track area
- Shopping destinations

Atlanta Motor Speedway

Inaugural year: 1960
Owner: Speedway Motorsports Inc. (SMI)
City: Hampton, Georgia
Size: 1.54 miles
Banking: 24 degrees
Grandstand seating capacity: 124,000
Past winners: Carl Edwards, Jimmie Johnson, Jeff Gordon, Bobby Labonte,
   Kevin Harvick, Dale Earnhardt Jr.
Most wins: Dale Earnhardt Sr. (8)

Track Contact Information

770-946-4211
www.atlantamotorspeedway.com

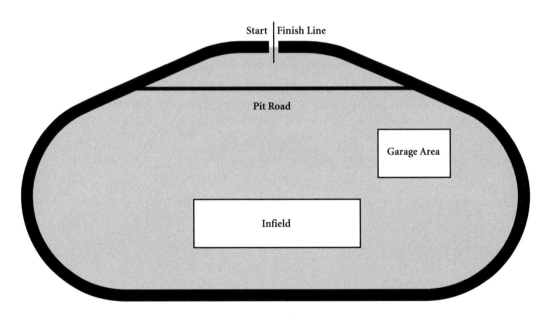

Hotels

Holiday Inn Express 770-461-5600
Best Western 770-898-1006
Courtyard by Marriott 404-607-1112
Four Seasons 404-881-9898
Hampton Inn 404-872-3234

Airports

Hartsfield International Airport
    404-530-6830
Tara Field 770-946-3153

Chamber of Commerce

Henry County Chamber of
    Commerce
    www.henrycvb.com
    770-957-5786

Track Area Hospitals

Henry Medical Center
    1010 Hospital Drive
    Stockbridge, GA
    770-506-1390
Spalding Regional Hospital Center
    601 South 8th Street
    Griffin, GA
    770-228-2721

Shopping

Southlake Mall
    1000 Southlake Mall Road
    Morrow, GA
    770-961-1050

Drivers' Wives' Favorite:

Worth the drive to Atlanta—
Lenox Square and Phipps Plaza

Dining

Applebee's 770-507-7201
Buffalos Café 770-389-6561
Outback Steakhouse 770-507-4198
Chili's 770-603-9900
Olive Garden 770-968-4800

Bristol Motor Speedway

Inaugural year: 1961
Owner: SMI
City: Bristol, Tennessee
Size: .533 miles
Banking: 36 degrees
Grandstand seating capacity: 160,000
Past winners: Kurt Busch, Tony Stewart, Elliot Sadler, Dale Earnhardt Jr., Jeff Gordon
Most wins: Darrell Waltrip (12)

Track Contact Information

423-764-1161
www.bristolmotorspeedway.com

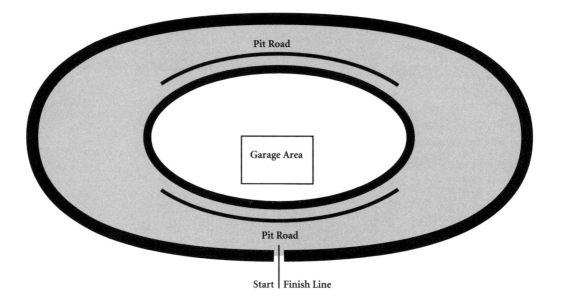

Hotels

Best Western 423-968-1101
Carnegie Hotel 423-979-6400
Courtyard by Marriott 276-591-4400
Doubletree Inn & Suites 423-929-2000
Fairfield Inn by Marriott
    423-282-3335

Airports

Tri-Cities Regional Airport
    423-325-6000

Chamber of Commerce

Bristol Chamber of Commerce
    www.bristolchamber.org
    423-989-4850

Track Area Hospitals

Wellmont Regional Medical Center
    1 Medical Park Blvd.
    Bristol, TN
    423-000-1111
Bristol Regional Medical Center
    1 Medical Park Blvd. #1
    Bristol, TN
    423-844-4200

Shopping

Bristol Mall
    500 Gate City Highway
    Bristol, VA
    276-466-8331
Market Street Center
    3900 Bristol Highway
    Johnson City, TN
    423-929-2766

Dining

Carrabba's Italian Grill 423-232-2858
Chops 276-466-4100
Cracker Barrel 423-323-9212
NASCAR Café 423-282-9223

California Speedway

Inaugural year: 1997
Owner: International Speedway Corporation (ISC)
City: Fontana, California
Size: 2 miles
Banking: 14 degrees in Turns 1–4 and 11 degrees in tri-oval
Grandstand seating capacity: 92,000
Past winners: Jeff Gordon, Elliott Sadler, Kurt Busch, Jimmie Johnson
Most wins: Jeff Gordon (3)

Track Contact Information

800-944-7223
www.californiaspeedway.com

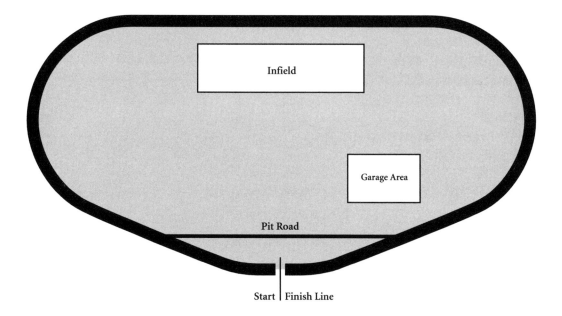

Hotels

Baymont Inn & Suites 909-987-5940

Hilton San Bernardino 909-889-0133

Marriott 951-784-8000

Pacific Palms Conference Resort
626-854-2419

Residence Inn by Marriott
909-937-6788

Airport

Ontario International Airport
909-937-2700

Chamber of Commerce

Fontana Chamber of Commerce
www.fontanacofc.org
909-822-4433

Track Area Hospitals

Arrowhead Regional Medical Center
400 North Pepper Avenue
Colton, CA
909-387-8111

Arrowhead Family Health Center
16854 Ivy Avenue
Fontana, CA
909-422-8029

Shopping

Fashion Plaza
17059 Valley Blvd.
Fontana, CA
909-428-0766

Inland Center Mall
500 Inland Center Drive
San Bernardino, CA
909-884-7268

Drivers' Wives' Favorite:

Worth the drive to L.A.—
Rodeo Drive

Dining

Rosa's 909-937-1220

Wolfgang Puck's Café 909-987-2299

Dave & Buster's 909-987-1557

New York Grill 909-987-1928

TGI Friday's 909-390-0050

Chicagoland Speedway

Inaugural year: 2001
Owner: Raceway Associates
City: Joliet, Illinois
Size: 1.5 miles
Banking: 18 degrees in turns; 11 degrees in tri-oval
Grandstand seating capacity: 75,000
Past winners: Kevin Harvick, Ryan Newman, Tony Stewart
Most wins: Kevin Harvick (2)

Track Contact Information

815-727-7223
www.chicagolandspeedway.com

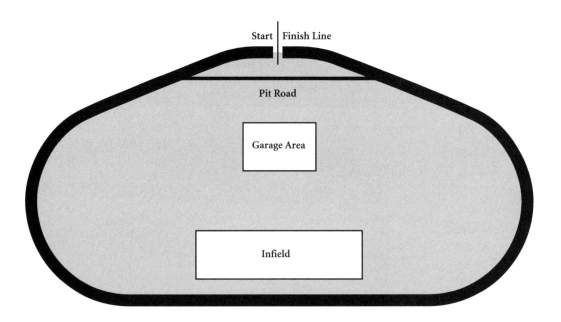

Hotels

Chicagoland Speedway and its surrounding community have joined forces to develop a reservation system for accommodations during race weekend. Visit www.chicagolandspeedway.com for a listing of all hotels participating in the community program.

Airports

O'Hare 773-686-2200
Midway 773-838-0600
Lewis University 815-588-0586
Joliet Park District 815-741-7267

Chamber of Commerce

Heritage Corridor CVB
www.heritagecorridorcvb.com
815-727-2323

Track Area Hospitals

Silver Cross Hospital
1200 Maple Road
Joliet, IL
815-740-1100
Palos Family Health Center
15327 West 143rd Street
Homer Glen, IL
708-301-4925

Shopping

Park Place Plaza
805 West Jefferson Street
Shorewood, IL
815-729-1383

Louis Joliet Mall
3340 Mall Loop Drive
Joliet, IL
815-439-1000

Dining

Lone Star Steakhouse 815-436-7600
Texas Roadhouse 815-577-9003
Fuji Japanese Steak House
708-403-1580
Buca di Beppo 708-349-6262
Bob Evans 815-725-0160

Darlington Raceway

Inaugural year: 1950
Owner: ISC
City: Darlington, South Carolina
Size: 1.366 miles
Banking: 25 degrees in Turns 1 and 2; 23 degrees in Turns 3 and 4
Grandstand seating capacity: 60,000
Past winners: Jimmie Johnson, Jeff Gordon, Terry Labonte, Ricky Craven, Jeff
   Burton, Sterling Marlin, Dale Jarrett, Ward Burton
Most wins: Dale Earnhardt Sr. and David Pearson (9)

Track Contact Information

866-459-7223
www.darlingtonraceway.com

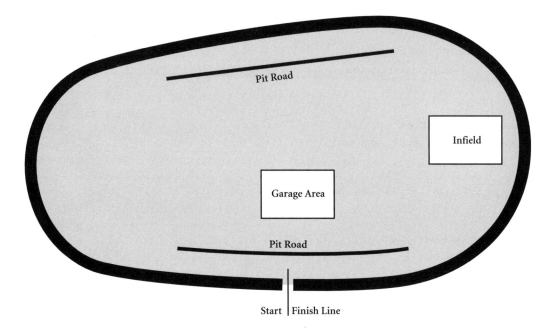

Hotels

Best Western 843-678-9292
Fairfield Inn 843-669-1666
Hampton Inn Suites 843-629-9900
Holiday Inn Express 843-664-2400
Wingate Hotel 843-629-1111

Airports

Darlington County Airport
    843-398-2987
Florence Airport Commission
    843-669-5001

Chamber of Commerce

Darlington County Visitor Bureau
    www.darlingtoncounty.org
    843-332-6401

Track Area Hospitals

Regency Hospital
    805 Pamplico Highway
    Florence, SC
    843-661-3499
Carolina Pines Regional
    1304 West Bobo Newsom Highway
    Hartsville, SC
    843-339-2100

Shopping

Florence Commons
    2835 David McLeod Blvd.
    Florence, SC
    843-661-0820
Magnolia Mall
    2701 David McLeod Blvd.
    Florence, SC
    843-669-0100

Dining

Cromer's Pizza 843-393-3626
Michael's Italian 843-669-3771
Raceway Grill 843-393-9212
Joe's Grill 843-393-9140

Daytona International Speedway

Inaugural year: 1959
Owner: ISC
City: Daytona Beach, Florida
Size: 2.5 miles
Banking: 31 degrees in turns; 18 degrees in tri-oval
Grandstand seating capacity: 168,000
Past winners: Dale Earnhardt Jr., Michael Waltrip, Jeff Gordon, Dale Jarrett,
    Sterling Marlin, Jeff Burton, Greg Biffle
Most wins: Richard Petty (10)

Track Contact Information

386-253-7223
www.daytonainternationalspeedway.com

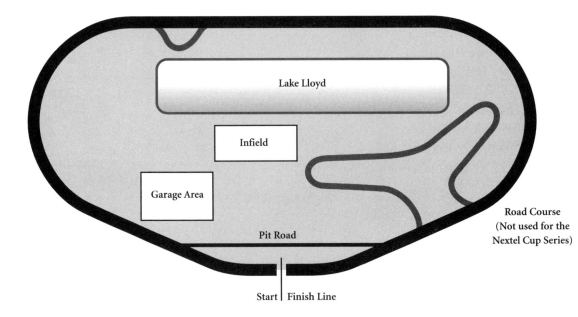

Hotels

Adams Mark Hotel 386-254-8200
Daytona Beach Hilton 386-767-7350
Hampton Inn 386-257-4030
Oceans Resorts, Inc. 386-257-1950
Ramada Inn Speedway 386-255-2422

Airports

Daytona Beach International Airport
    386-248-8030
Orlando International Airport
    407-825-2355

Chamber of Commerce

Daytona Beach Chamber of
    Commerce
    www.daytonachamber.com
    800-854-1234

Track Area Hospitals

Halifax Medical Center
    303 North Clyde Morris Blvd.
    Daytona Beach, FL
    386-254-4000
Crosslin Health Center
    714 Dr. Mary McLeod
    Bethune Blvd.
    Daytona Beach, FL
    386-239-6198

Shopping

Volusia Mall (directly across the street
    from the speedway)
    386-253-6783

Worth the Walk

During Speed Weeks many drivers make appearances at the Volusia Mall due to the fact that radio and TV stations broadcasts live from the center court area.

Dining

Down the Hatch 386-761-4831
Outback Steakhouse 386-253-6283
Julian's 386-677-6767
Carrabba's Italian Grill 386-255-3344

Dover International Speedway

Inaugural year: 1969

Owner: Dover Downs Entertainment Incorporated

City: Dover, Delaware

Size: 1 mile

Banking: 24 degrees

Grandstand seating capacity: 140,000

Past winners: Ryan Newman, Jimmie Johnson, Jeff Gordon, Dale Earnhardt Jr., Tony Stewart, Dale Jarrett, Ricky Rudd

Most wins: Richard Petty and Bobby Allison (7)

Track Contact Information

800-441-7223

www.doverspeedway.com

Hotels

Dover Downs Hotel and Conference
   Center 866-473-7378
Fairfield Inn 302-677-0900
Hampton Inn 302-736-3500
Holiday Inn Express 302-678-0600
Sheraton 302-678-8500

Airports

Philadelphia International Airport
   215-937-6937
Baltimore/Washington International
   Airport 800-435-9294

Chamber of Commerce

Central Delaware Chamber of
   Commerce
   www.cdcc.net
   302-734-7513

Track Area Hospitals

Kent General Hospital
   540 South Governors Avenue
   Dover, DE
   302-744-7400
Bayhealth Medical Center
   640 South State Street
   Dover, DE
   302-674-4700

Shopping

Dover Mall
   1365 North Dupont Highway
   Dover, DE
   302-734-0415

Blue Hen Mall
   655 South Bay Road
   Dover, DE
   302-678-2209

Dining

Shucker's Pier 13 302-674-1190
Roma Italian Restaurant
   302-678-1041
The Lobby House 302-741-2420
Atwood's 302-674-1776
Village Inn 302-734-3245

Homestead-Miami Speedway

Inaugural year: 1995
Owner: ISC
City: Homestead, Florida
Size: 1.5 miles
Banking: 18 to 20 degrees, variable
Grandstand seating capacity: 65,000
Past winners: Tony Stewart, Greg Biffle, Bobby Labonte, Kurt Busch, Bill
    Elliott
Most wins: Tony Stewart (2)

Track Contact Information

305-230-7223
www.homesteadmiamispeedway.com

Start | Finish Line

Pit Road

Lake

Garage Area

Lake

Hotels

Biltmore Hotel 305-445-1926
Doubletree Grand Hotel
    305-372-0313
Holiday Inn Resort & Marina
    305-451-2121
Loews Miami Beach Hotel
    305-604-1601
Miami Beach Ocean Resort
    305-534-0505

Airports

Miami International 305-876-7000
Fort Lauderdale International
    954-359-1200
Homestead General 305-247-7757
Tamiami Executive Airport
    305-869-1700

Chamber of Commerce

Homestead/Florida City Chamber of
    Commerce
    www.chamberinaction.com
    423-989-4850

Track Area Hospitals

Homestead Hospital
    160 NW 13th Street
    Homestead, FL
    786-243-8000
Jackson South Community Hospital
    959 North Krome Avenue
    Homestead, FL
    305-245-4022

Shopping

Cutler Ridge Mall
    20505 South Dixie Highway
    Miami, FL
    305-235-8562
Prime Outlets at Florida City
    250 East Palm Drive
    Homestead, FL
    305-248-4727

Drivers' Wives' Favorite:

Worth the drive to Miami—more shopping than one credit card should allow.

Dining

Capri 305-247-1542
Christy's 305-446-1400
Farmer's Market 305-242-0008
Keys Seafood House 305-247-9456
Tiffany's 305-246-0022

Indianapolis Motor Speedway

Inaugural year: 1994
Owner: The Hulman/George family
City: Indianapolis, Indiana
Size: 2.5 miles
Banking: 9 degrees
Grandstand seating capacity: 250,000
Past winners: Jeff Gordon, Kevin Harvick, Ricky Rudd, Dale Jarrett, Bobby
    Labonte
Most wins: Jeff Gordon (4)

Track Contact Information

317-492-6700
www.indianapolismotorspeedway.com

Hotels

Adam's Mark 317-248-2481
Baymont Inn 317-244-8100
Comfort Inn West 317-487-9800
Radisson Garden Inn 317-244-3361
Quality Inn and Suites 317-381-1000

Airports

Indianapolis International Airport
    317-487-9594

Chamber of Commerce

Indianapolis Convention and Visitors
    Association
    www.indy.org
    317-639-4282

Track Area Hospitals

Indiana University Hospital
    550 University Blvd.
    Indianapolis, IN
    317-274-5000
Regenstrief Health Center
    1050 Wishard Blvd.
    Indianapolis, IN
    317-630-7860

Shopping

Lafayette Square Mall
    3919 Lafayette Road
    Indianapolis, IN
    317-291-6390

Dining

Average Joe's Sports Pub
    317-253-5844
Buffalo Wild Wings 317-241-9464
Hard Rock Cafe 317-636-2550
Old Spaghetti Factory 317-635-4725
Rock Bottom Brewery & Restaurant
    317-681-8180

Infineon Raceway

Inaugural year: 1989
Owner: SMI
City: Sonoma, California
Size: 1.99-mile road course (11 turns)
Banking: Varying degrees of banking throughout
Grandstand seating capacity: 30,000
Past winners: Jeff Gordon, Robby Gordon, Ricky Rudd, Tony Stewart
Most wins: Jeff Gordon (4)

Track Contact Information

800-870-7223
www.infineonraceway.com

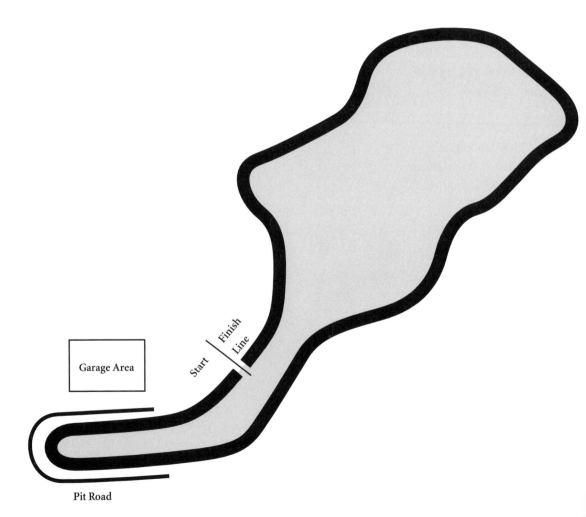

Hotels

Best Western Novato Oaks Inn
    800-625-2466
Courtyard by Marriott 415-925-1800
DoubleTree Hotel 800-222-8733
Embassy Suites 800-EMBASSY
MacArthur Place Hotel 707-938-2929

Airports

San Francisco International Airport
    650-821-8211
Oakland International Airport
    510-563-3300
Sacramento International Airport
    916-929-5411
Napa Airport 707-253-4300

Chamber of Commerce

Sonoma Valley Chamber of
    Commerce
    www.sonomachamber.com
    707-996-1033

Track Area Hospitals

Sonoma Valley Hospital
    347 Andrieux Street
    Sonoma, CA
    707-935-5000
Queen of the Valley Hospital
    1100 Trancas Street
    Napa, CA
    707-257-4062

Shopping

Napa Premium Outlets
    629 Factory Stores Drive
    Napa, CA
    707-226-9876

Drivers' Wives' Favorite:

Worth the drive to Sonoma—Sonoma Square, a quaint village of merchants nestled in downtown Sonoma. Even though you are deep in the wine country, the boutique-style shopping has down-home southern warmth and charm.

Dining

Deuce 707-933-3823
Murphy's Irish Pub 707-935-0660
La Salette 707-938-1927
Piatti 707-996-2351
Saddles 707-933-3191

Kansas Speedway

Inaugural year: 2001
Owner: ISC
City: Kansas City, Kansas
Size: 1.5 miles
Banking: 15 degrees
Grandstand seating capacity: 80,187
Past winners: Ryan Newman, Jeff Gordon, Joe Nemechek
Most wins: Jeff Gordon (2)

Track Contact Information

913-328-7223
www.kansasspeedway.com

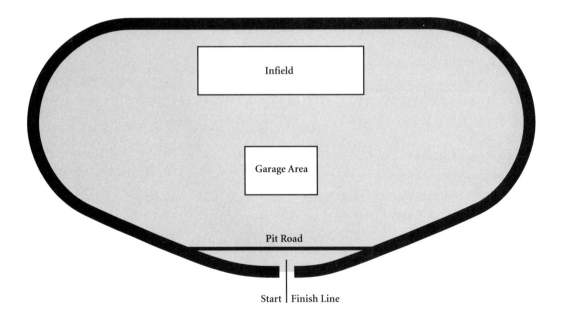

Hotels

Chateau Avalon 913-596-6000

Fairfield Inn Overland Park
913-381-5700

Four Points Barcelo Hotel
816-753-7400

Great Wolf Lodge 913-299-7001

Hyatt Regency Crown Center
816-421-1234

Airports

Kansas City International Aiport
816-243-5237

Chamber of Commerce

www.kansascity.com

www.visitkc.com

Track Area Hospitals

Bethany Medical Center
51 North 12th Street
Kansas City, KS
913-281-8400

Truman Medical Center
2310 Holmes
Kansas City, MO
816-556-3159

Shopping

Indian Springs Shopping Center
4601 State Avenue
Kansas City, KS
913-287-9393

Everett Mall
920 Main Street
Kansas City, MO
425-347-2756

Dining

Hereford House Restaurant
816-842-1080

Plaza III 816-753-0000

River Market Brewing Co.
816-471-6300

Sutera's West Restaurant
913-721-5549

WJ McBride's Irish Pub & Restaurant
913-788-7771

Las Vegas Motor Speedway

Inaugural year: 1998
Owner: SMI
City: Las Vegas, Nevada
Size: 1.5 miles
Banking: 12 degrees
Grandstand seating capacity: 137,000
Past winners: Matt Kenseth, Jeff Burton, Sterling Marlin, Jeff Gordon
Most wins: Jeff Burton and Matt Kenset (2)

Track Contact Information

800-644-4444
www.lvms.com

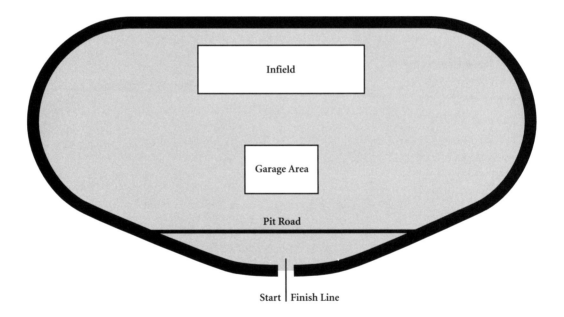

Infield

Garage Area

Pit Road

Start | Finish Line

Hotels

Aladdin Resort 702-785-5555

Hard Rock Hotel 702-693-5000

Imperial Palace Hotel-Casino
702-731-3311

Luxor Hotel-Casino 702-262-4444

Sun Coast Resorts 702-636-7111

Airports

McCarran International Airport
702-261-5211

Chamber of Commerce

Las Vegas Convention and Visitors
Authority
www.lasvegas24hours.com
702-892-7575

Track Area Hospitals

Valley Hospital Medical Center
620 Shadow Lane
Las Vegas, NV
702-388-4000

Jean Hanna Clark Health Center
1001 Shadow Lane
Las Vegas, NV
702-388-3500

Shopping

Las Vegas Premium Outlets
875 South Grand Central Parkway
Las Vegas, NV
702-474-7500

R & R Ultimate Mega Mall
1231 Wizard Avenue
North Las Vegas, NV
702-631-5590

Meadows Mall
4300 Meadows Lane
Las Vegas, NV
702-878-4849

Dining

Battista's Hole in the Wall
702-732-1424

Buca di Beppo 702-866-2867

Lawry's The Prime Rib 702-893-2223

Rosewood Grill 702-792-9099

Triple Brew Pub 702-387-1896

Lowe's (Charlotte) Motor Speedway

Inaugural year: 1960
Owner: SMI
City: Concord, North Carolina
Size: 1.5 miles
Banking: 24 degrees
Grandstand seating capacity: 171,000
Past winners: Jimmie Johnson, Tony Stewart, Matt Kenseth, Jamie McMurray, Sterling Marlin, Jeff Burton, Jeff Gordon
Most wins: Darrell Waltrip and Bobby Allison (6)

Track Contact Information

800-455-3267
www.lowesmotorspeedway.com

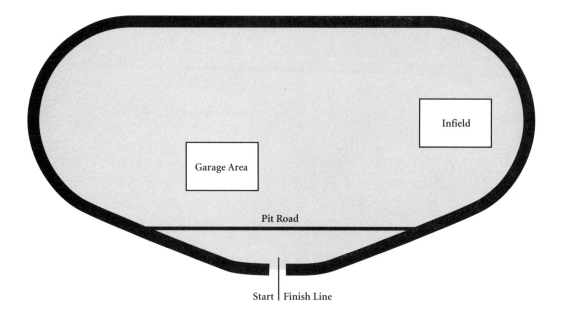

Hotels

Courtyard by Marriott 704-549-4888
Hampton Inn Suites 704-979-5600
Hilton Charlotte at University Place
704-547-7444
Sleep Inn & Suites 704-979-8800
Spring Hill Suites by Marriott
704-979-2500

Airports

Charlotte/Douglas International
Airport 704-359-4013
Concord Regional Airport
704-793-9000

Chamber of Commerce

Charlotte Convention and Visitors
Bureau
www.charlottecvb.org
704-334-2282

Track Area Hospitals

NorthEast Medical Center
920 Church Street North
Concord, NC
704-786-1144
University Hospital
8800 North Tryon Street
Charlotte, NC
704-548-6000

Shopping

Concord Mills Outlet Mall
8111 Concord Mills Blvd.
Concord, NC
704-979-3000

Carolina Mall
1480 US Highway 29 North
Concord, NC
704-786-1185

Dining

Kabuto Japanese Steakhouse
704-548-1219
Macado's 704-979-3700
Razoo's Cajun Grill 704-979-0222
The Italian Oven 704-795-6836
The Speedway Club 704-455-3216

Martinsville Speedway

Inaugural year: 1956
Owner: ISC
City: Martinsville, Virginia
Size: .526 miles
Banking: 12 degrees
Grandstand seating capacity: 91,000
Past winners: Jeff Gordon, Jimmie Johnson, Dale Jarrett, Kurt Busch, Bobby
    Labonte, Tony Stewart, Ricky Rudd
Most wins: Darrell Waltrip (11)

Track Contact Information

877-722-3849
www.martinsvillespeedway.com

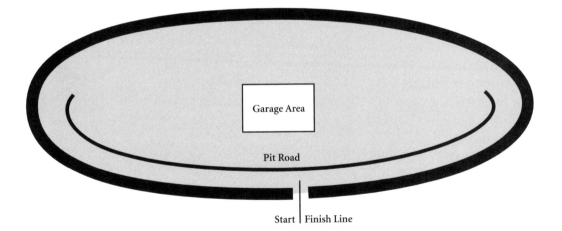

Hotels

Best Western 276-632-5611

Best Lodge 276-647-3941

Days Inn 276-638-3914

Hampton Inn 276-647-4700

Holiday Inn Express 276-666-8888

Airports

Blue Ridge Airport 276-957-2291

Piedmont Triad International Airport
    336-665-5666

Chamber of Commerce

Martinsville Henry County Chamber
    of Commerce
    www.mhcchamber.com
    276-632-6401

Track Area Hospital

Martinsville Memorial Hospital
    320 Hospital Drive
    Martinsville, VA
    276-666-7200

Shopping

Liberty Fair Mall
    240 Commonwealth Blvd.
    Martinsville, VA
    276-666-2340

Dining

Clarence's Steakhouse 276-956-3400

Elizabeth's Pizza 276-647-3859

Hurley's Uptown Pub 276-632-4444

Texas Steakhouse 276-632-7133

Yamato Japanese Steakhouse
    276-638-2743

Michigan International Speedway

Inaugural year: 1969
Owner: ISC
City: Brooklyn, Michigan
Size: 2 miles
Banking: 18 degrees
Grandstand seating capacity: 136,373
Past winners: Ryan Newman, Greg Biffle, Tony Stewart, Jeff Gordon, Kurt
　　Busch, Dale Jarrett, Matt Kenseth
Most wins: David Pearson (9)

Track Contact Information

800-354-1010
www.mispeedway.com

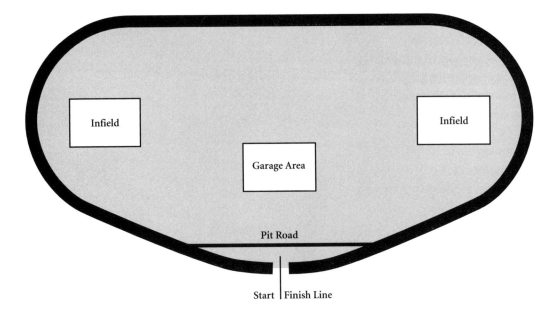

Hotels

Clearwater Hotel 517-547-7472
Country Inn & Suites 734-529-8822
Doubletree Hotel 734-467-8000
Evans Lake Resort 517-431-2233
Governor's Inn and Conference
    Center 517-393-5500

Airports

Detroit Metro Airport 734-247-7678
Reynolds Field/Jackson 517-788-4225
Shamrock Airport/Brooklyn
    517-592-6253

Chamber of Commerce

Brooklyn Chamber of Commerce
    www.brooklynmi.com
    517-592-8907

Track Area Hospital

Addison Community Hospital
    421 North Steer Street
    Addison, MI
    517-547-6152

Shopping

Westwood Mall
    1850 W. Michigan Avenue
    Jackson, MI
    517-787-1170
Jackson Crossing Mall
    1092 Jackson Crossing
    Jackson, MI
    517-783-4890

Dining

The Beach Bar 517-529-4211
Daryl's Downtown 517-782-1895
Hunt Club 517-782-0375
Poppa's Place 517-592-4625
The Common Grill 313-475-0470

New Hampshire International Speedway

Inaugural year: 1993
Owner: Bob Bahre
City: Loudon, New Hampshire
Size: 1.058 miles
Banking: 12 degrees
Grandstand seating capacity: 91,000
Past winners: Kurt Busch, Jimmie Johnson, Jeff Burton, Jeff Gordon, Ryan Newman, Tony Stewart, Robby Gordon
Most wins: Jeff Burton (4)

Track Contact Information

603-783-4931
www.nhis.com

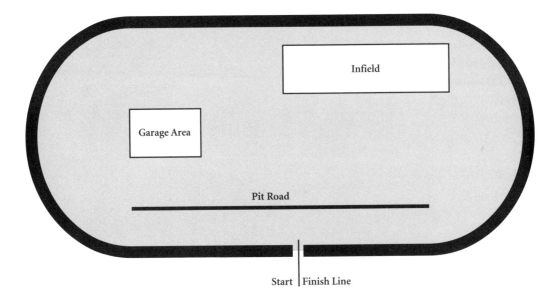

Start | Finish Line

Hotels

Courtyard by Marriott 603-225-0303
The Gunstock Inn 603-293-2021
Misty Harbor Resort 603-293-4500
Naswa Resort 603-366-4341
Sheraton Four Points 603-668-6110

Airports

Concord Airport 603-228-2267
Manchester Airport 603-624-6539
Laconia Airport 603-524-5003

Chamber of Commerce

Greater Concord Chamber of
    Commerce
    www.concordnhchamber.com
    603-224-2508

Track Area Hospitals

New Hampshire Hospital
    36 Clinton Street
    Concord, NH
    603-271-5300
Concord Hospital
    250 Pleasant Street
    Concord, NH
    603-225-2711

Shopping

Steeplegate Mall
    270 Loudon Road
    Concord, NH
    603-224-1523
The Mall of New Hampshire
    1500 South Willow Street
    Manchester, NH
    603-669-0434

Dining

Boar's Tavern 603-798-3737
Egg Shell Restaurant 603-783-4060
The Green Martini 603-223-6672
Makris Lobster & Steak House
    603-225-7665
Sandy Point Restaurant
    603-875-6001

Phoenix International Raceway

Inaugural year: 1988
Owner: ISC
City: Avondale, Arizona
Size: 1 mile
Banking: 11 degrees in Turns 1 and 2; 9 degrees in Turns 3 and 4
Grandstand seating capacity: 76,812
Past winners: Dale Earnhardt Jr., Matt Kenseth, Jeff Burton, Tony Stewart,
    Dale Jarrett
Most wins: Jeff Burton, Dale Earnhardt Jr., and Davey Allison (2)

Track Contact Information

602-252-2227
www.phoenixintlraceway.com

Start | Finish Line

Pit Road

Garage Area

Infield

Hotels

Desert Garden Corporate Suites
800-935-6479
Gold Spur Ranch 623-932-9307
Hilton Suites—Downtown
602-222-1111
Quality Hotel & Resort 602-248-0222
The Wigwam Resort 623-935-3811

Travel

Sky Harbor International Airport
602-273-3300

Chamber of Commerce

Phoenix Chamber of Commerce
www.phoenixcvb.org
877-225-5749

Track Area Hospital

West Valley Emergency
Center & Hospital
13677 West McDowell Road
Goodyear, AZ
623-245-6700

Shopping

Desert Sky Mall
7611 West Thomas Road
Phoenix, AZ
623-245-1400
Maryvale Mall
5035 West Camelback Road
Phoenix, AZ
602-272-0421

Dining

Driver's Sports Grill 623-536-8571
Pinnacle Peak Patio 602-585-1599
Raul & Teresa's Restaurant
623-932-1120
Stuart Anderson's Black Angus
602-245-1644
T-Bone Steakhouse 602-276-0945

Pocono Raceway

Inaugural year: 1974
Owner: Pocono Raceway Inc. (the Mattioli family)
City: Long Pond, Pennsylvania
Size: 2.5 miles
Banking: 14 degrees in Turn 1; 8 degrees in Turn 2; 6 degrees in Turn 3
Grandstand seating capacity: 70,000
Past winners: Jimmie Johnson, Ryan Newman, Jeremy Mayfield, Tony
   Stewart, Jeff Gordon, Dale Jarrett, Bobby Labonte
Most wins: Bill Elliott (5)

Track Contact Information

570-646-2300
www.poconoraceway.com

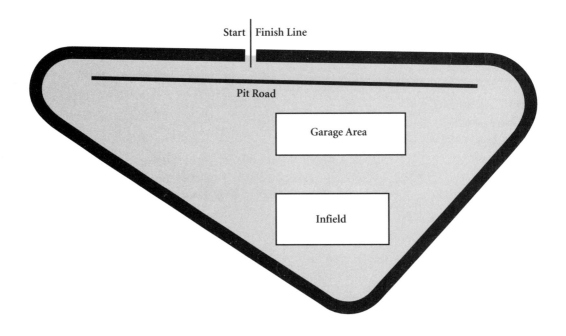

Hotels

Best Western 570-646-6000
The Chateau at Camelback
  570-629-5900
Mt. Laurel Resort 570-443-8411
Split Rock Resort 570-722-9111
Woodlands Resort 570-824-9831

Airports

Wilkes-Barre/Scranton International
  (AVP) 877-235-9287
LeHigh Valley International Allentown
  (ABE) 800-359-5842

Chamber of Commerce

Pocono Mountains Vacation Bureau
  www.800poconos.com
  800-POCONOS

Track Area Hospitals

Community Medical Care
  663 Pocono Blvd.
  Mt. Pocono, PA
  570-839-8691
St. Luke's Hospital
  Route 209S
  Gilbert, PA
  610-681-2337

Shopping

Stroud Mall
  Route 611
  Stroudsburg, PA
  570-424-2770

Pocono Village Mall
  301 Route 940
  Mt. Pocono, PA
  570-839-6409

Dining

Bailey's 570-839-9678
Beaver House 570-424-1020
High Elevations 570-443-8899
Robert Christian's 570-646-0433
Velma's 570-839-7386

Richmond International Raceway

Inaugural year: 1953
Owner: ISC
City: Richmond, Virginia
Size: .75 mile
Banking: 14 degrees
Grandstand seating capacity: 105,000
Past winners: Dale Earnhardt Jr., Ryan Newman, Jeremy Mayfield, Tony
 Stewart, Jeff Gordon, Dale Jarrett
Most wins: Richard Petty (9)

Track Contact Information

804-345-7223
www.rir.com

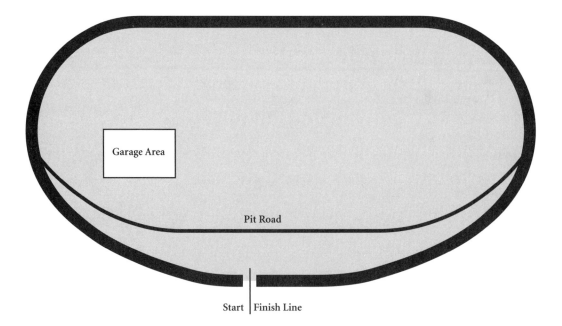

Hotels

Best Western Hanover House
 804-550-2805
Crowne Plaza Richmond
 804-780-0900
Doubletree at Richmond Airport
 804-226-6400
Embassy Suites West 804-672-8585
Hilton Garden Inn 804-521-2900

Airports

Richmond International Airport
 804-226-3000
Richmond Jet Center 804-226-7200

Chamber of Commerce

Richmond Visitors Bureau
 www.richmondva.org
 888-RICHMOND

Track Area Hospitals

Sheltering Arms
 2805 West Broad Street
 Richmond, VA
 804-915-1174
Cumberland Hospital
 2811 Moss Side Avenue
 Richmond, VA
 804-228-2280

Shopping

Beaufort Mall
 7134 Midlothian Pike
 Richmond, VA
 804-745-8255
Sixth Street MarketPlace
 550 East Marshall Street
 Richmond, VA
 804-648-6600

Drivers' Wives' Favorite:

Worth the drive to downtown Richmond—quaint, boutique-style shops.

Dining

Buffalo Wild Wings 804-672-8732
Firebird's Rocky Mountain Grill
 804-364-9744
La Petite France 804-353-8729
Pasta Luna 804-762-9029
The Tobacco Company Restaurant
 804-782-9555

Talladega Superspeedway

Inaugural year: 1969

Owner: ISC

City: Talladega, Alabama

Size: 2.66 miles

Banking: 33 degrees in turns; 18 degrees in tri-oval

Grandstand seating capacity: 143,000

Past winners: Dale Earnhardt Jr., Michael Waltrip, Jeff Gordon, Bobby Labonte, Dale Jarrett

Most wins: Dale Earnhardt Sr. (10)

Track Contact Information

877-462-3342

www.talladegasuperspeedway.com

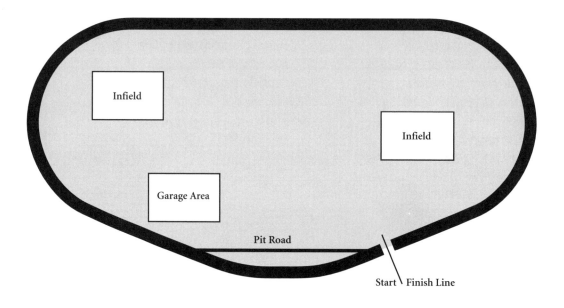

Hotels

Best Western of Oxford/Anniston
256-831-3410
Comfort Inn 256-831-0860
Executive Inn & Suites 205-763-9777
Holiday Inn Express 256-832-4041
The Wingate Inn 256-831-1921

Airports

Anniston: Anniston Municipal Airport
256-831-4410
Atlanta: Hartsfield International
Airport 404-530-6830
Birmingham: Birmingham
International Airport 205-595-0533
Talladega: Talladega Municipal
Airport 256-761-4815

Chamber of Commerce

Talladega Chamber of Commerce
www.talladegachamber.com
256-362-9075

Track Area Hospital

Citizens Baptist Medical Center
604 Stone Avenue
Talladega, AL
256-362-8111

Shopping

Quintard Mall
700 Quintard Drive
Oxford, AL
256-831-4180

Drivers' Wives' Favorite:

Worth the drive to Birmingham—
Riverchase Galleria.

Dining

Café Avanti 205-338-8900
Matehuala Mexican Restaurant
256-362-5754
Old Smokehouse Bar-B-Q
256-237-5200
Parigi's Pizza 256-362-3313
Western Sizzlin' 205-814-5665

Texas Motor Speedway

Inaugural year: 1997
Owner: SMI
City: Fort Worth, Texas
Size: 1.5 miles
Banking: 24 degrees
Grandstand seating capacity: 154,861
Past winners: Elliott Sadler, Ryan Newman, Dale Earnhardt Jr., Jeff Burton, Matt Kenseth, Dale Jarrett
Most wins: No multiple race winners

Track Contact Information

817-215-8500
www.texasmotorspeedway.com

Start | Finish Line

Pit Road

Garage Area

Hotels

Candlewood Suites 817-838-8229
Doral Tesoro 817-961-0800
Gaylord Texan Resort 817-778-1000
Hilton Garden Inn 817-222-0222
Renaissance Worthington
    817-870-1000

Airports

Dallas/Fort Worth International
    Airport 972-574-8888
Love Field 214-670-6073

Chamber of Commerce

Fort Worth Convention and
    Visitors Bureau
    www.fortworth.com
    817-336-8791

Track Area Hospitals

John Peter Smith Hospital
    1500 South Main Street
    Fort Worth, TX
    817-429-5156
Baylor All Saints Medical Center
    1400 8th Avenue
    Fort Worth, TX
    817-926-2544

Shopping

Sundance Square
    512 Main Street
    Fort Worth, TX
    817-339-7777
Ridgemar Mall
    1888 Green Oaks Road
    Fort Worth, TX
    817-731-6591

Dining

Angeluna 817-334-0080
Cattleman's Steak House
    817-624-3945
Lonesome Dove Western Bistro
    817-740-8810
Saltgrass Steakhouse 817-306-7900
Texas de Brazil 817-882-9500

Watkins Glen International

Inaugural year: 1986 (raced on three different occasions in 1957, 1964, and
    1965)
Owner: ISC
City: Watkins Glen, New York
Size: 2.45-mile road course
Banking: 6 to 10 degrees, variable
Grandstand seating capacity: 41,000
Past winners: Jeff Gordon, Tony Stewart, Robby Gordon, Ricky Rudd
Most wins: Jeff Gordon (4)

Track Contact Information

866-461-7223
www.theglen.com

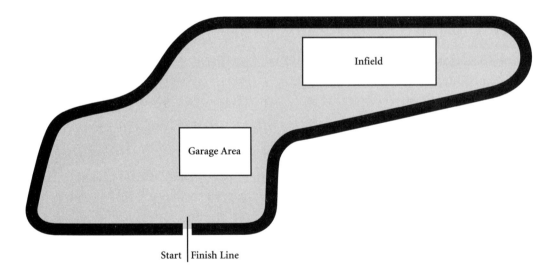

Hotels

Best Western Lodge on the Green
607-962-2456
Country Inn & Suites 607-739-9205
Fairfield Inn 607-937-9600
Hilton Garden Inn 800-445-8667
Holiday Inn Corning 607-962-5021

Airports

Elmira-Corning Regional Airport
607-739-5621
Greater Rochester International
Airport 716-464-6010
Syracuse Hancock International
Airport 315-454-3263
Tompkins County Airport
607-257-0456

Chamber of Commerce

Watkins Glen Chamber of Commerce
www.schuylerny.com
607-535-4300

Track Area Hospital

Schuyler Hospital
220 Steuben Street
Montour Falls, NY
607-535-7121

Shopping

Arnot Mall
3300 Chambers Road
Horseheads, NY
607-739-8704

Consumer Square Mall
830 County Road 64
Elmira, NY
607-796-5268

Dining

Grapevine Deli and Café
607-535-6141
Jerlando's Pizza Co. 607-535 4254
Market Street Brewing Company
607-936-2337
Palm's Restaurant 607-734-5599
Wildflower Café 607-535 9797

Glossary

The NASCAR Dictionary

Aerodynamics—The effect of air moving across, over, under, and around the race car.

Air pressure—The force exerted by air against the inner walls of a tire.

Alternator—A device mounted on the engine that keeps the battery charged while the engine is running. The alternator has a belt, referred to as the alternator belt.

Appearance—When a driver shows up at an event or car lot, grand opening event, convention, etc., to sign autographs and meet fans.

Apron—A portion of track that separates the racing section of the track from the grass of the infield.

Associate sponsor—A company that does not choose or is not able to fund a primary sponsorship. These companies get less exposure for their dollar. A team can have many associate sponsors.

Autograph—A signature from someone famous.

Backstretch—The long straight portion of a racetrack located farthest from the grandstands.

Banking—The degree of angle of the track surface.

Bite/Round of bite—The result of adjusting the jacking screws at each wheel, which adds or reduces pressure on a large spring that transfers weight from corner to corner of the car. Teams do this to help the tires stick to the track better.

Blocking—Keeping another driver from passing.

Body—The skin or metal covering of the car.

Camber—The amount of positive or negative angle of the tire from vertical.

Carburetor—An engine part that controls the air and fuel mixture supplied to the engine.

Car chief—The crew chief's right-hand man.

Champion—A driver who has won the NASCAR Cup Series title.

Chassis—The steel frame of the car.

Crankshaft—The shaft that delivers power from the pistons to the transmission.

Crew chief—The leader of the pack . . . the race team boss.

Deck lid—The metal casing that covers the trunk.

Doughnuts—A stunt move a driver does when he wins a race. This is a circular motion on the track that leaves skid marks in the shape of a doughnut.

Down force—The result of air flowing across the body of the car, pressing it down onto the track.

Draft—The hole in the air made by a car. A car utilizing the draft runs in the hole in the air left by the car running in front of it, thereby conserving gas and reducing stress on the engine.

Drafting—When cars race together to achieve faster speeds.

Drag—The effect of the car going through the air. The less drag on the body of the car, the faster it will go.

Dynometer (dyno)—A machine used to measure an engine's horsepower.

Equalized tire—When the air pressure is the same in the inner and outer liner of a tire. An equalized tire causes a vibration that can be felt by the driver.

Frame—The chassis of the race car.

Frontstretch—The straight portion of the track surface located in front of the main grandstands and flag stand.

Fuel cell—Fuel tank.

Fuel pump—The car part that pumps fuel from the fuel cell to the carburetor.

Garage area—The secured area where the cars are kept and worked on throughout race weekend. You must have a special pass to enter the garage area.

Greenhouse—The structure that covers the upper area of a race car, which includes the area extending from the base of the windshield on the front of the car, across the tops of the doors to the base of the window in the rear.

Handling—How a car behaves on the track. If a driver has handling issues, his car does not race well.

Happy Hour—The last official practice before the start of the race.

Hauler—Every team has an eighteen-wheeler truck that transports the race cars from one track to another, which team members refer to as the hauler. Teams use the hauler as a meeting place on race weekends. This is where many tools and equipment are stored.

Horsepower—The amount of engine power a car has. Horsepower is measured by the amount of power it takes to move 33,000 pounds one foot in a minute.

Intermediate track—A racetrack that measures over a mile but less than two miles.

Interval—The distance between cars on the track. This is measured by car lengths or seconds.

Jet dryer—A machine used to dry the track surface quickly when Mother Nature rains down. Also known as a "turbo blower."

Lug nuts—Nuts used to attach the tire to the race car. The lug nuts are applied with a special air wrench during pit stops. Each tire has five lug nuts on each wheel.

Marbles—Excess tire rubber found at the edge of the racetrack.

Modern era—NASCAR's modern era dates from 1972 to the present.

Paint scheme—The artwork on a race car. Some drivers have special paint schemes for special events.

Pit pass—A pass that allows the pass holder to enter the pit stall areas. A pre-race pit pass allows the pass holder to tour pit road before the start of the race. A "hot pass" allows the pass holder to stay in the pit during the race event.

Pit road—The road where pit crews service their cars.

Pit stall—The designated area for each team to service its car.

Pit stop—When a car enters pit road and comes to a stop in its specific pit stall to be serviced.

Pit wall—The wall that separates the pit stall area from pit road.

Pit window—An estimated number of laps a team feels their driver can run before coming in for a pit stop. This changes at every track due to track size.

Pole position—The number one starting spot; the fastest qualifier.

Primary sponsor—A team's main sponsor; the most noticeable sponsor you see when you look at the car, and also the most expensive.

Provisional—A spot that allows a driver to compete in a race when he or she did not qualify on time. This is awarded to past champions and top drivers in points.

Quarter panel—The metal on both sides of the race car from the rear bumper below the deck lid to over the wheel well.

Relief driver—A driver standing by to replace the original driver in case of illness or injury. All relief drivers must be approved by NASCAR.

Restart—The restarting of the race after a caution period.

Restrictor plate—A metal plate that restricts the air flow from the carburetor to the engine. Restricting the air flow slows down the car. Restrictor plates are used at Daytona and Talladega.

Road courses—Tracks that have both left and right turns, as opposed to the normal left-turn mode of the non-road-course tracks. Infineon and Watkins Glen are the Cup Series road course tracks.

Roll cage—The steel frame that surrounds a driver in the cockpit area. This cage protects the driver if the car should roll or flip, as well as from a side impact.

Roof flaps—Flaps that lie flat on the top of the car unless the car spins or moves in an abrupt manner. The flaps are designed to help keep cars from going airborne.

RPMs—Revolutions per minute; the speed an engine is turning.

Scanners—Radio-type instruments that allows a listener to pick up on radio conversations between a team and driver.

Scuffs—Tires that are not new but usually have not been used for more than five laps.

Setup—The way in which a car is mechanically set up to race and/or qualify.

Short track—A track that is less than one mile in length.

Show cars—In most cases, old race cars that are not used for competition anymore, and are now used for appearance events, corporate events, etc. Each show car has a driver who transports the car from one event to another.

Silly season—A time during the season when rumors start escalating about where certain drivers will go (with what team) for the following season. This usually starts about halfway through the season.

Stickers—New tires; tires that have the manufacturer's stickers still attached, meaning they've never been used.

Superspeedway—A track measuring more than two miles in length.

Tachometer—An instrument in a race car to help drivers determine pit road speed by displaying the engine's RPMs. It is also used to optimally gear the car.

Transponder—A device that sends an electronic signal to wires buried in a race car. The device monitors lap times and assists in electronically scoring the cars.

Trunk lid—The rear deck lid.

Victory Lane—Where the winning driver and team go to celebrate their win.

Wedge—The cross-weight adjustment of a race car. Basically, putting more weight on the wheel by compressing the spring that corresponds to that corner of the car.

Window net—A mesh net that covers the driver's window area.

Wind tunnel—A research facility that simulates the effects of air passing over and around a car like those encountered during normal racing situations.

NASCAR Slang

Battling for position—Two or more cars jockeying for position on the track.

Behind the wall—Taking the race car off of pit road to either the garage area or behind the pit wall.

Blowing an engine, or blowing up—When an engine expires or will not work anymore . . . a car cannot go without a working engine.

Brake check—When a driver hits his brakes just enough to make the car behind him touch the brakes. The brake-checking car then hits the gas pedal in a quick fashion. For example, on a race restart, a driver hits his brakes, messing up the timing of the car behind him and giving him a jump on everyone. *Remember, no brake lights!*

Brushing (or tapping) the wall—When a driver slightly brushes against the wall, with little to no damage.

Bump draft—When a car running in the draft bumps the rear bumper of the car in front of him—a nudge. The "bump" is used to give the other car a little boost, although some drivers use it as a warning to the car on the receiving end to get it moving.

Clean air—Air that does not have turbulence from other race cars. If a driver comments that his car runs better in clean air, he basically means his car performs better out front.

Girlfriend to Girlfriend

If you want to be a NASCAR fan you have to learn the language. Once you learn the language . . . it's time to put your new skills to the test.

Cookie-cutter track—A track that is not unique; nothing special. The "cookie-cutter" comparison comes from the idea of a track developer basically using a cut-out mold of a track to form a new track, making the track surface and shape the same as other tracks.

Develops a push—Same as **tight**. See **Tight out.**

Dirty air—A term used for turbulent air caused by fast-moving cars, which can be good or bad. Some drivers feel a particular car may run better in dirty air.

Gas and go—When a driver comes in for a pit stop to get gas but no tires.

Going a lap down—A car that is close to being lapped; not scored on the lead lap.

Green flag conditions—This means the track is ready to race, contains no debris, etc.

Hitting your marks—Visual marks a driver makes at a track to help him know when to accelerate, let off gas, or pass. Each driver has specific things they use for marks, such as the flag stand or a certain marking on a portion of the wall.

Hung out to dry—A driver who gets out of the racing line or draft and quickly loses position on the track.

Lapped traffic—Cars that are not on the lead lap and are usually much slower than the lead pack.

Lead pack—The lead cars running in a pack of cars.

Loose in—When the rear of the car feels like it is unstable, loose, or squirmy; a common complaint from the drivers.

On the lead lap—Cars scored on the lead lap; cars not laps down.

Out front—Racing at the front of the other cars, in the lead.

Race ready—A car that is ready to race.

Racing groove—Where the drivers want to race on certain tracks. It is like the highway versus a side road. The high groove will take a driver closer to the outside wall, whereas the lower groove will be closer to the bottom end of the track. Some tracks have more than one groove. Tracks can change over time—a one-groove track can become a two-groove track.

Right off the truck—A race car that needs no work, changes, etc. before hitting the track. Drivers use this term when a car runs well and has required no significant changes from the race shop to the track.

Round of wedge—An adjustment of the pressure on the rear springs of the wheels.

Running wide open—Pushing the accelerator to the floor.

Seasoned track—A track that has had years of racing on it; a mature track surface.

Splash of gas—When the gas man only gives the driver enough gas to finish the race. You see this happen at the end of a race when track position is crucial.

Stop and go—A penalty NASCAR hands out to drivers who speed on pit road. The driver must enter the pit stall during an unscheduled pit stop and come to a complete stop (one full second) before the NASCAR official will allow the car to exit back onto the track.

Tail of the longest line—A penalty in which a driver is sent to the end of the longest line of cars for the restart of the race.

Tight out—A car feels tight when the front tires will not turn well, making it tough to hold the car in the turns; also, when the driver must turn the steering wheel more than the front of the car actually turns.

Trading paint—When drivers show aggressive driving techniques toward one another; lots of bumping and banging. Basically, putting one car's paint on another from close racing; rubbing is racing.

Venue—A place that houses an event, used generically. For example, Lowe's Motor Speedway is a racing venue.

Most Commonly Asked/ "Lost the Nerve" Questions

1. Why do race cars drive counterclockwise?

There is no certain explanation for why the drivers and tracks favor the left turn. However, many drivers believe that because they sit on the left side of the car it makes sense to turn left—constant right turns would be awkward for them. The exception to this would be road racing, which includes turns to the right, although the turns are not a constant or continuous turning motion, which makes them less awkward.

2. How does a race car driver get noticed by a Cup car owner?

The best way to get discovered by a Cup car owner is to first and foremost build up an impressive racing résumé. No car owner will take a driver seriously if he or she does not have some racing experience. It does not have to be experience in any of NASCAR's top three levels of racing, but you must have local racing—and winning—experience. Once you have a good résumé, you start contacting teams about development programs. Many teams, like Roush Racing, actually hold tryouts for up-and-coming drivers. Some teams have scouts who travel to local tracks around the country looking for the next big star. As with anything, many times it is who you know. Seek out everybody you know in the business to ask for assistance or information. The harder you work at it, the better chance you have of getting a break.

3. What do drivers do when they have to use the bathroom?

The last thing a driver does before a race is go to the bathroom. Under normal circumstances the conditions in a race car are far from desirable—meaning hot temperatures, cramped quarters, etc. Drivers normally sweat so much that using the bathroom is the furthest thing from their minds. However, there are exceptions . . .

Bobby Allison and Tony Stewart both experienced urgent bathroom situations while leading races. Both drivers felt that the need to win was more important than the need for a bathroom. Both drivers went on to win their respective races but dismissed themselves from the Victory Lane celebration. Get my drift?

Tina Gordon completed an ARCA event at Talladega in 2001 only to tell the reporter (who happened to be me) on national television that she had to pee really bad and went on to thank the ladies waiting for the restroom for allowing her to cut in line.

4. How do the drivers stay cool in the car if it does not have air-conditioning?

Each driver uses a small refrigeration unit called a "cool box." This contraption funnels air from the outside through a small hose straight into the driver's helmet, keeping his face and head cool. It is believed that if a driver's head and face stay cool, his entire body stays cool.

5. How do crew members and drivers identify themselves to track security?

All drivers, crew members, NASCAR officials, and drivers' wives must have a NASCAR license. License holders are required to wear a badge at all times; most choose to display them around their necks. The hard card credentials issued to drivers, crew members, spouses, and NASCAR officials are nontransferable and are quite expensive. Each hard card credential is paid for by the team or, in some cases, the individual.

6. Why do drivers swerve their cars during caution laps?

They swerve to ensure that the tires are clean of any debris that may have been picked up during the caution period, and if the tires are new, it warms them up.

7. Why do cars make pace laps before the start of the race?

The pace laps are to warm up the tires and the engine for the race. Pace laps also serve as a good indicator to the drivers of pit road speed. Remember, the cars do not have speedometers but tachometers. The pace car rides along at exactly the pit road speed in front of the pits to ensure that the drivers have a good tachometer reading.

8. How did most of the drivers' wives meet their husbands?

The majority of the wives met or knew their husbands very early in their careers. Some of the drivers have known their wives since they were kids. The last couple of years have actually brought more young drivers to the sport who are unattached. Go get 'em, girls!

9. Where can I find out about jobs in NASCAR?

There is no absolute answer to this, other than that you have to be where the action is. Most race teams are based in and around the Charlotte, North Carolina, area. Getting your foot in the door is the hardest part. Many Cup-level teams will only hire candidates with experience. A great route is to seek out jobs with Busch- and Truck-level teams to gain valuable experience. Once you have some résumé material, you will have a better chance at landing a Cup Series position. Be leery of people and services that make promises attached to a fee. Remember, if it sounds too good to be true, then it probably isn't true. Always ask for documented placement success and professional references if you decide to go that route. There are also several technical schools in North Carolina that specialize in race team training. This is more for crew members than drivers.

10. Are drivers considered athletes?

This is one of the oldest and most heated debates in NASCAR. Some argue that drivers are not athletes because all they do is sit in a car all day and drive around in circles. The clincher is that drivers have to be in tip-top shape and have the stamina of a freight train to make it through an entire race. The amount of physical strength and concentration would certainly justify race car drivers being called athletes.

11. Is it impossible to get "noticed" by a driver or to be asked out on a date?

Impossible . . . no, but unlikely is more like it. If you don't have four tires and average 180 mph, it will be hard to get noticed. The most difficult thing would be meeting the driver first and foremost and then having the one-on-one time to get the driver's attention. The drivers will tell you flat out that the single major reason for not having a significant other is the time factor. Drivers have very little time to do anything outside racing, including date. Don't get me wrong, it obviously happens, but you better hope fate is on your side.

12. Do race car drivers ever get scared?

Yes, but race car drivers do not admit fear. Some call it respect, others call it acceptance, but in the end there is always a level of fear. There is an age-old saying in the garage area that "if a driver develops fear, they should walk away from the sport." There have been many drivers who hung up their helmets for good out of nothing but fear.

NASCAR
Trivia Answers

1. What driver has the most Daytona 500 wins?

Richard Petty—7 total

2. What track hosted the race dubbed "One Hot Night" in 1992?

Lowe's Motor Speedway in Charlotte, North Carolina

3. What former Cup Series driver nicknamed Cup Series regular Joe Nemechek "Front Row Joe"?

NBC/TNT's Wally Dallenbach

4. What veteran driver was nicknamed "Mr. September"?

Harry Gant

5. How many Daytona 500 starts did it take Darrell Waltrip to finally win the coveted trophy?

17

6. What current Cup-level car owner participates in amateur boxing in his off time?

Ray Evernham

7. What driver is known as "Rocket Man"?

Ryan Newman

8. What current driver endorses Halston Z-14 cologne?

Jeff Gordon

9. Who are the founders of the Victory Junction Gang Camp?

Kyle and Pattie Petty

10. What track hosts the Gatorade Duals?

Daytona

11. What is the nickname of car owner Jack Roush?

The Cat in the Hat

12. What Cup Series competitor is also known as "Smoke"?

Tony Stewart

Few women have covered the sport of auto racing at the level of LIZ ALLISON. Liz has spent seventeen years at the racetrack, first as the wife of racing superstar Davey Allison until his untimely death in 1993, and later as a member of the sports media covering NASCAR Nextel Cup events.

Liz's passion for the sport continues today as she covers stock car racing through many facets of the media. She is a popular radio personality in Nashville, Tennessee, and her insight and top-notch guests have made her program the number one NASCAR show in Nashville. She has hosted such television shows as ESPN2's *Motoring Music City*, as well as served as a race analyst for the CBS affiliate in Nashville.

In 2004, Liz joined the Nashville Superspeedway as their first female announcer and host for the speedway's four major racing events each year. Liz has covered NASCAR racing for TNT Sports as a pit road reporter and feature reporter, and has appeared on many national television and radio shows. *The Girl's Guide to NASCAR* is her fourth published book on the sport, and she serves as a contributing author to many racing publications. She is remarried and lives in Nashville with her husband, Ryan, and three children.